TALKING
WITH GOD

Books in the Woman's Workshop Series

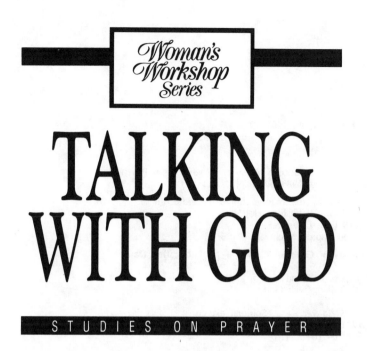

Woman's Workshop Series

TALKING WITH GOD

STUDIES ON PRAYER

GLAPHRÉ

ZondervanPublishingHouse

Grand Rapids, Michigan

A Division of HarperCollinsPublishers

TALKING WITH GOD: A WOMAN'S WORKSHOP ON PRAYER
Copyright © 1985 by Glaphré Gilliland

Requests for information should be addressed to:
Zondervan Publishing House
1415 Lake Drive, S.E.
Grand Rapids, Michigan 49506

Library of Congress Cataloging in Publication Data

Glaphré Gilliland.
    Talking with God.

    1. Prayer.   2. Spiritual exercises.   I. Title.
BV210.2.G58   1984   248.3'2   84-25804
ISBN 0-310-45341-0

All Scripture quotations, unless otherwise noted, are taken from the HOLY BIBLE: NEW INTERNATIONAL VERSION (North American Edition). Copyright © 1973, 1978, 1984 by the International Bible Society. Used by permission of Zondervan Bible Publishers.

Scripture quotation marked (TLB) are taken from *The Living Bible,* copyright © 1971 by Tyndale House Publishers, Wheaton, Illinois. Those marked (NASB) are taken from the *New American Standard Bible,* the Lockman Foundation, © 1972, LaHabra, California.

Field of Wild Poppies by Claude Monet
Cover Photo by SUPERSTOCK INTERNATIONAL
Cover Design by *The Church Art Works,* Salem, Oregon

Edited by Christy Elshof and Janet Kobobel

Printed in the United States of America

91   92   93   94   95 / CH / 16   15   14   13   12

TO MY MOM,
FLOY GILLILAND
Whose selfless love and positive belief
is a part of all God does
in and through me.

CONTENTS

INTRODUCTION

What will help you toward a better prayer life? First, you must want a more meaningful, a more effective life of prayer. Second, you must pray. The old adage "practice makes perfect" carries an element of truth as it relates to prayer. Prayer brings us closer to God—opening our spirits to think His thoughts, to feel His concerns, and, as we yield our wills to Him, to become more like the perfect "pray–er," Jesus Christ.

This book is written to help you increase the desire and the discipline necessary to grow in the area of prayer. *Talking with God* was written to be a practical workshop. At the end of each chapter are personal devotions ("Personal Discoveries in Prayer") and group discussions ("Shared Discoveries in Prayer"). The book is most effective when used in this combination—personal devotions followed by group discussion. However, *Talking with God* also makes a valuable personal study.

If you choose to study this book alone, use the "Personal Discoveries in Prayer" as directed. Then use the "Shared Discoveries in Prayer" as a personal devotion as well, taking several days to cover the content. Some questions designed for a group may not apply: simply move on to the next question. You can benefit greatly, even apart from a group discussion.

Are you ready to begin a more exciting life—a life in which you become closer to your Creator, and more positively and vitally involved in the lives of others? Then, begin *Talking with God*. But be aware, the more open your communication with God becomes, the more your life can change—for the better.

—Janet Kobobel
Editor

1

CAN PRAYER REALLY HELP?

They arrived at the same time . . . in different cars.

They were a success—

in business,

in popularity,

in community achievements—but not in their marriage.

I watched as this middle-aged couple walked up my sidewalk and greeted each other stiffly. The nine-month separation that had invaded their twenty-year marriage had bred an awkwardness between them.

As they sat in my living room, Richard and Linda told me their story: The open hurting of unmet needs.

The clamoring tension of desperation.

The bleeding from gouging each other with the jagged edges of past failures.

"We're tired of trying," admitted Richard. "We've been to a marriage counselor, *and* a psychologist."

"We've tried everything we know to do," added a weary Linda. "We've talked to all our church friends. . ."

"And talked and talked and talked!" jabbed Richard. Linda flinched at her husband's reminder of her readiness to talk of his indiscretion.

"But," Richard said, "we thought before we call it quits we might as well try prayer. It's our last resort. What do you think? Can prayer really help?"

It wasn't a new question. Neither was it a new situation. And there was no uncertainty in my answer—no lack of belief in its validity. Just the haunting reminder of how often we wait for the sinking point of a crisis before we turn to God for help.

Some of us have seen so few positive results from our prayers that gradually—often without even realizing it— we've come to the very private conclusion that prayer doesn't help all that much. Not really. Not in any reliable way.

Oh, it's not a conclusion we shout out in church. It's not a conclusion we share readily with our friends. We may not even admit it to ourselves. But believing it does have a profound effect on our lives, and tragically, we usually don't realize our loss.

Most of us have comfortably relegated prayer to either brief thoughts tossed casually at God or to desperate pleas in the midst of traumatic ordeals. We fervently *wish* prayer could help . . . but we don't *believe* it will. Instead we secretly decide that prayer—the wondrous kind we hear about—is for *other* people. Or perhaps we think that some magical moment will come that will create within us a deep desire to pray, give us a wonderfully fulfilling discipline of prayer, and begin a tremendously successful prayer life.

But prayer is *not* just for other people. It's not to be put on hold until we are wiser and more disciplined. There's no magical moment waiting to transform all of life into a glorious level of godly fellowship.

The tendency for most of us is to talk about the importance of prayer more than we actually pray. We tell people we'll pray for them, but we don't usually follow through on that promise. We say we believe in prayer . . . but give little time to it.

We all make time for those things we consider vital: sleep, work, eating, family. It's not enough to simply say we believe in prayer. The time we actually spend in prayer tells the true story of how much we think prayer helps.

If we're to believe, really believe, that prayer can help, we have to rediscover some truths about prayer—discover them as if we've never heard them before. We must discover them not just intellectually, not just to explain to others, but in ways that change our prayer time with God.

GOD SAYS PRAYER HELPS!

If you don't believe prayer can help you in some area of life, or don't believe it as much as you need to, then try this:

1. Begin with an honest request:

"God, I don't believe prayer helps. I'm sorry, but I don't. Please, God, create within me a belief in prayer." Or, "God, I do believe prayer helps. But, please, God, create within me a greater belief in prayer. *Help me to believe and feel about prayer the way You intended me to believe and feel.*"

2. Listen to what God says:

> "Look to the Lord and His strength, seek His face always" (1 Chron. 16:11).
>
> "Devote yourselves to prayer, being watchful and thankful" (Col. 4:2).

It's easy to breeze through these Scriptures, missing their meaning. Remember, these are not just *words*. We have to think about what God is saying to *us*, tell God our feelings about these prayer Scriptures, and ask His help.

God never made prayer an option. We have to believe that! If we don't, then that's where we start:

> "God, help me understand how important prayer is to You, and how important it's supposed to be to me."

3. Look to Jesus:

> "But Jesus often withdrew to lonely places and prayed" (Luke 5:16).

> "Very early in the morning, while it was still dark, Jesus got up, left the house and went off to a solitary place, where He prayed" (Mark 1:35).

If Jesus—God's Son, miraculous Teacher, Savior of the world—prayed, how much more do we need to draw close to the Father?

4. Ask God to help you believe in prayer:

Search out the Scriptures that tell of people praying. As you read them, ask God to increase your faith.

> "When the people cried out to Moses, he prayed to the Lord and the fire died down" (Num. 11:2).

> "Elijah was a man just like us. He prayed earnestly that it would not rain, and it did not rain on the land for three and a half years. Again he prayed, and the heavens gave rain and the earth produced its crops" (James 5:17–18).

To believe prayer really can make a difference, we must use the very vehicle of fellowship we are doubting: "God, help me believe in prayer."

> God the Father loves us enough to accept us with our doubts.

God the Healer will heal the damage to our faith that
was created each time we prayed and saw no results.
God the Teacher will instruct us about prayer.
God the Guide will lead us into a belief that

PRAYER CAN HELP!

That belief is the beginning—the beginning of an intimate fellowship with God that changes so much in life, including us.

It was one of those brisk spring days when you're sure you hear birds happily chirping even when there are no birds around. People greeted each other warmly as they got out of their cars and walked up to the third house on the right. It wasn't a new house, but there was something new about the people who lived there.

The couple stood with their arms around each other and shared about God's healing. Friends cried as they heard how God helped this couple stop attacking each other, look to God, and bridge the aching gap between them.

Three years after that joyous meeting in their home, this couple says their marriage is more fulfilling, more fun than it had ever been. Ask Richard and Linda *now* if prayer can really help.

> "They will call on My name, and I will answer them."
> (Zech. 13:9b).

PERSONAL DISCOVERIES IN PRAYER

(You may find the table of contents at the front of your Bible helpful in finding the Scriptures in this devotional.)

1. Read Luke 18:1.

2. Rewrite Luke 18:1, inserting your name in place of the word "men."

   _____

   _____

   _____

3. Tell God your feelings about prayer in general and about your personal prayer life. Write some of those thoughts here:

   _____

   _____

   _____

   _____

   _____

4. Ask God to help you feel about prayer the way He wants you to.

5. Read 1 Chronicles 16:11.

6. Rewrite 1 Chronicles 16:11, inserting your name, as if God is speaking to you personally.

   _____

   _____

7. Ask God to help you believe more strongly than ever that prayer makes a difference.

8. Read 2 Kings 4:32–34.

9. Allow God to bring to your mind times when He has helped you or people you have known or heard about. As you recall these times of special help, make note of

them. Allow God to create new faith within you concerning His special provision of prayer.

_____

_____

_____

_____

10. Read Luke 11:1.

11. Ask God to teach you to pray.

SHARED DISCOVERIES IN PRAYER

A. As an entire group:

1. Each pray silently, asking God to teach you in this workshop.

2. Each pray silently for the person to your right. Ask God to use this study in her life.

3. 1 Chronicles 16:11.

   a. What does this verse mean to you? How do you "seek God"?

   _____

   _____

   _____

   b. What significance does the word "always" have?

   _____

   _____

   _____

4. 2 Chronicles 7:14. According to this Scripture, what does God want for us besides forgiveness of sins?

_____

_____

_____

5. 2 Chronicles 7:17–18. What role would prayer have had in the things God told Solomon to do in verse 17?

_____

_____

_____

_____

_____

6. Psalm 50:14–15. (If different translations are available, have several read.)

   a. What is the part prayer plays in the two instructions given in verse 14?

   _____

   _____

   _____

   _____

   b. What part does prayer play in verse 15?

   _____

   _____

   _____

   _____

   _____

7. Luke 5:16; 6:12; 22:41–44.

a. What importance did Jesus place on prayer?

_____

_____

_____

b. Why did Jesus need to pray?

_____

_____

_____

_____

c. What does Jesus' prayer life say to us about our need to pray?

_____

8. Each pray silently, asking God to increase your belief in His power to answer your prayers.

9. Have several share past answers to prayer in their lives or the lives of others.

10. Each pray silently.

a. Thank God for these answers to prayer.

b. Again, ask God to increase your belief in prayer.

B. In groups of two or three people:

1. Each share a problem you have in the area of prayer that you'd like help with during these weeks of study.

2. Pray for each other about these prayer problems. (Each group of two or three decide whether this prayer will be silent or aloud.)

3. Share with others in your group a time you prayed for something important, and God didn't seem to answer.

4. Pray for each other: Ask God to heal any damage done by His seeming unresponsiveness and to free the person to believe that God does work through her prayers. (Again, each group decide if these prayers will be aloud or silent.)

2

SECURE IN THE RELATIONSHIP

In the midst of a group of energetic children sat a small, fragile girl. The group enthusiastically responded to the Children's Prayerlife Seminar, but this girl's gaze stayed fixed on the floor. As I taught these fun-filled cherubs, I prayed for the little one who never looked up.

After the session, Amy's eyes darted away quickly when I spoke to her. That night I asked God to minister to this frightened girl with the sad eyes: "God, most of all, help her be secure with *You*. Help her be comfortable talking to You. And, please help her feel comfortable with others, too."

The next day, I greeted Amy before the seminar. She smiled! She smiled at the *floor*, but it was still a smile.

Toward the end of the session, Amy participated in a group discussion. The next day she volunteered for a role play the kids acted out in front of the group. "She must have been more timid than frightened," I thought. And I thanked God for helping her. Amy gave me a big hug before she left that day.

That night Amy's parents talked to me. "We're having trouble believing the difference in our daughter," Amy's dad said. "It's only been three days! How could so much happen in three days?"

"Amy has always been a fearful child," her mom added. "She never talks to anyone except family, and not very much to us." Her voice was shaking as she told of the psychologists and psychiatrists, and Amy's inability to attend public school because of her fear.

"After the second day of the seminar, Amy asked to say the blessing before supper, and she prayed with me before she went to bed," her dad continued with excited disbelief. "That's never happened before! Tonight she talked all through dinner and said she was in a play today. Was she really?"

I assured him that she was.

"How?" asked Amy's mom. "How could she change so quickly? What made her feel so secure?"

"Only God could bring about such a rapid change," I answered. "But, a child often understands quickly that *in God is great security*. Once someone feels the security of belonging to God and talking with Him, that security spreads to other relationships."

The three of us thanked God for beginning to heal Amy's fear.

Whether or not we feel secure with people and changing circumstances, *we can feel secure in the relationship we have with God.*

God wants us to.

We need to.

True praying . . . with freedom . . . with abandon . . . is difficult without that security. How can we trust ourselves, our dreams, our hurts, our loved ones to Someone with whom we don't feel safe?

> " . . . Let the beloved of the Lord rest secure in Him . . . "
> (Deut. 33:12).

Wherever we are in our Christian walk, the more secure we are in our relationship with God, the more trusting our times of prayer will be.

BELONGING TO GOD BRINGS SECURITY

There's a special, warm feeling you get when you walk into your home after having been gone on a vacation. It's hard to put into words . . . it's just a wonderful feeling of belonging.

We experience that same feeling when something fits: a job, a climate, a friend, a memory, a church.

We were created to belong to God. It's *in Him*—in that relationship—that we discover our purpose, are equipped for that purpose, and are enabled to fulfill God's specific will for our lives. It's a wonderful place to be because *everything fits*.

It's much more than the relief of walking into our homes after spending weeks someplace else. It's more like never having had any family and then discovering that we have the most wonderful Father! A Father waiting to accept and love us.

But it's even more than that. The decision to belong to God, to become a Christian, washes away all the wrong we've ever done or thought. It makes us new. Clean. Free. It's the beginning.

> "If we confess our sins, He is faithful and just and will forgive us our sins and purify us from all unrighteousness." (1 John 1:9).

To belong to God: we ask His forgiveness for the wrong or sins in our life; we tell God we want to be His child; and God, through Jesus Christ, lovingly forgives us. Then that wondrous grace of God moves in and adopts us into His family.

We belong!

Oh, the security!

"Now all praise to God for His wonderful kindness to us and His favor that He has poured out upon us, because we belong to His dearly loved Son" (Eph. 1:6, TLB).

IF YOU'RE NOT SURE . . .

Sometimes a person thinks she's a Christian, thinks she belongs to God . . . but she's not sure. Although we may grow in our desire for God and we may become more aware of our need for God's forgiveness, we can't grow into belonging to Him. We don't belong to God because we believe He exists, or because we get goose bumps when we hear a hymn or because we enjoy attending church.

Belonging to God is a decision.

A deliberate, thought-through decision.

Some of us made that decision so long ago we've forgotten what an awesome relationship we have. We take belonging to God for granted. To enjoy the security that comes from belonging to God, we need to reflect on what that belonging means.

Belonging to God . . . we were created for it! It brings a security that frees us to develop an intimate fellowship of prayer with our Father.

"And you also are among those who are called to belong to Jesus Christ" (Rom. 1:6).

JESUS—THE WAY—GIVES SECURITY

Jesus says, "I am the Way." He is! The way to receive forgiveness from God. The way to establish fellowship with God.

> "Jesus answered, 'I am the way and the truth and the life. No one comes to the Father except through me.' " (John 14:6).

Jesus continues to be our Way, for He is praying for us— even now. What security!

> "Christ Jesus, who died—more than that, who was raised to life—is at the right hand of God and is also interceding for us" (Rom. 8:34).

Jesus gives us the privilege of praying in His name. It's in Jesus' name that we come to God in prayer—for Jesus made that relationship possible.

The phrase "in Jesus' name" is not just to be used with "Amen" to conclude a prayer. It's not just a way to say, "I'm through now, God." To ask a particular request "in Jesus' name" carries a very serious responsibility. We are saying, "God, to the best of my understanding, this is a prayer Jesus wants."

> "You did not choose me, but I chose you to go and bear fruit—fruit that will last. Then the Father will give you whatever you ask in my name" (John 15:16).

Oh, the love, the security that comes from having such a provision, such a Way!

GOD'S LOVE GIVES SECURITY

A young woman meticulously clears a place on the closet shelf for a small box. She puts the container in its prepared spot with great care. After all, the delivery man said it held a treasure—a treasure that would change her life.

But not yet. She'd wait to open it.

When she was older.

One day while straightening her closet, she noticed the box. She hadn't thought of it for a long time. How could she have forgotten to open it? It was all hers!

But not yet.

When she had learned more.

As the years passed, whenever the woman felt lonely, she gently placed her hand on the lid of the small box . . . hoping to draw comfort from the hidden treasure. She longed to peek inside her box.

But not yet.

When she had done more to deserve it.

Years later, she was desperate. She took the box and put it on her dresser where she could look at it more easily. Oh, if only she could open it! How she needed some help!

But not yet.

When she wasn't so needy.

Bent with age, she pulled herself out of the chair and walked slowly to the dresser. With uncertainty she carefully opened the box—feeling she really had no right to the treasure hidden within.

Inside was a piece of paper yellowed with age. It read: "ADOPTION FINALIZED." The attached note said,

> "Dear One,
>
> This is My gift. The inheritance of being a loved and cared-for daughter. Please let me know if you accept My gift.
>
> Your new Father."

This particular story never happened. Yet, in a way, it happens over and over in our lives. One of the richest parts of the living inheritance God gives us is His love.

> God's love: Available. Consistent. Dependable. Unconditional. Personal. Proven. Trustworthy.

Because we know this wondrous, unexplainable inheritance has been delivered, we think we've opened the package and are benefiting from its transforming presence. But are we, really? Or do we look at it . . . refer to it . . . touch it . . . but never actually release it in the moments of our lives? Are we robbing ourselves of the personal reality of God's love?

> "God, I'm scared. Your Word says that means I don't believe You love me. Please, God, reassure me that You love me. Help me believe that *even in this situation* I can count on Your love." (See 1 John 4:18.)

> As God gently reaffirms His love for us,
>   security in the relationship returns,
>   and we are freed to pray for the problem with
>   real trust.

> "And so we should not be like cringing fearful slaves, but we should behave like God's very own children, adopted into the bosom of His family, and calling to Him, 'Father, Father' " (Rom. 8:15, TLB).

Your adoption is complete! You are not a foster child. You're not on probation. You have nothing to prove before you can receive God's love—it comes with the relationship. God's love isn't for later or when you're more worthy. You and I can never—not ever—do anything to deserve God's love.

But, you don't *earn* a gift . . .
    you *accept* it.

You can get to heaven without the fulfilling security of knowing how much God loves you. You can serve and minister to people without having that security. Ironically, you can even help others believe God loves them and yet never be totally sure of that love yourself.

But what a tragedy! What a waste.

    God *loves you*.
        Not because of what you can do.
        Not because of how you look.
        Not because of what you've accomplished.
        Not because of how good your past is.
          God loves you because you're His daughter.
          His love is your inheritance!

Don't wait until later to accept God's love.
    Embrace it.
        Be comforted by it.
          Be restored by it.
            Be fulfilled by it.
              Be secure in it!

"How great is the love the Father has lavished on us, that we should be called children of God! And that is what we are!" (1 John 3:11).

PERSONAL DISCOVERIES IN PRAYER

(This devotional may take more than one day to complete. Don't rush through; give yourself time to make it meaningful.)

    1. Read John 3:16–18.

a. Rewrite these verses, inserting your name whenever "whoever" or a similar word is used, so it reads as if God is speaking directly to you.

_____

_____

_____

_____

_____

_____

b. Ask God to give you a deeper understanding of these verses. Then read what you have just written.

c. *If you do not have a personal relationship with Jesus Christ as Savior, or are not sure if you do,* please seriously consider the following:

   (1) You were created to fellowship with God, to belong to God. That relationship is not possible without being adopted into God's family, and that adoption takes place through Jesus' gift of His life on the cross. It was in that act of God's love through Jesus that the price was paid for *your* sins. He did this so you wouldn't have to pay the price. He did this in place of *you,* for *you.*

   Jesus offers you this gift of salvation and the privilege of being God's daughter.

   You accept God's gift by asking His forgiveness for the wrongs in your life, for your sins. When you confess those wrongs, Jesus forgives them. After accepting God's forgiveness, tell God your desire to belong to Him and your belief that Jesus is

God's Son. You are at that moment as much God's daughter as someone who has belonged to Him for years. The adoption is complete!

(2) Think: Do you really want to continue your life without God? Or do you want to accept His sacrificial gift of love and salvation?

(3) Read Isaiah 1:18. This verse is God's personal invitation to you.

(4) If you want to become a Christian:

    (a) Right now tell God you are sorry for your sins—the wrong things and the wrong thoughts in your life.

    (b) Ask God's forgiveness for those sins.

    (c) Accept God's forgiveness, and thank Him for Jesus' death on the cross for your sins.

    (d) Tell God that you want to belong to Him and that you believe Jesus is His Son.

    (e) God has forgiven _____
                       (write in your name)
    of her sins. _____
                       (write in your name)
    belongs to God *now*.

    (f) Read 2 Corinthians 5:17, inserting your name as you read. Thank God that this Scripture is for *you*.

d. If *you are not sure you want a personal relationship with Jesus Christ as Savior*, consider the following:

(1) Ask God to help you sense the difference belonging to Him would make in your life.

(2) Ask God to help you believe *you need to belong to Him*.

e. If you *do have a personal relationship* with Jesus Christ:

(1) Think about God's gift of love through Jesus and tell God your feelings about it.

(2) Read 2 Corinthians 5:17.

(3) List some of the ways a personal relationship with Jesus Christ has made you a new or different person.

_____

_____

_____

_____

(4) Thank God for His personal gift of salvation. Thank Jesus for giving His life for *you*.

2. Read 1 John 4:18.

a. Rewrite it, inserting your name as if God is speaking directly to you.

_____

_____

_____

b. Ask God to teach you that He loves you.

c. Reread the verse you have just written.

(1) Allow God to help you think of any area of your life right now in which it's difficult to believe God loves you.

(2) Think of God's love.

(3) Think of God's love working in this area.

(4) Ask God to help you believe He loves you—even in *this* area.

d. Think of something loving that God has done for you and thank Him for it.

e. Ask God to teach you how much He loves you.

f. Think of something loving that God has done for a loved one and thank Him for it.

g. Ask God to teach you He loves you.

h. Thank God that He loves you even in those moments when you don't feel His love.

i. Ask God to teach you how much He loves you.

3. Read Psalm 23:1.

a. If possible, look out a window or take a walk and repeat this verse. Ask God to heal any emotional damage from the past when you didn't feel His love.

b. _____ is completely and totally
(write in your name)
loved by God. The adoption of _____
                                (write in your name)
into God's family is final!

c. Thank God for loving you.

d. Tell God of your love for *Him*.

SHARED DISCOVERIES IN PRAYER

A. As an entire group:

1. Everyone look up Ezekiel 37:23 and have one person read it aloud.

2. Discuss why God made provision to forgive our sins.

_____

_____

B. In groups of eight or ten people:

1. Read Isaiah 40:3–5.

2. As many as may wish to, share how God used someone in your life to prepare the way for you to become a Christian.

3. Read Isaiah 45:21–22.

4. Share: As many as wish to, share the circumstances surrounding your becoming a Christian.

5. As many as feel directed, pray aloud, expressing your gratitude to God for the people He used in your life before you were a Christian. Thank Him for salvation. Tell Him how you feel about belonging to Him.

C. As an entire group:

1. Read Isaiah 55:6–7 and 2 Corinthians 5:17.

2. Using one to three words, all who wish pray aloud: Thank God for some of the differences being a Christian has made in your life. (e.g. "God, thank You for peace.")

3. Read John 14:6–10.

4. Discuss

a. Why do we need to learn all we can about Jesus?

_____

_____

_____

b. According to this Scripture, what is the major way we get to know God better?

_____

_____

c. According to Jesus, who do we see when we look at Him? _____

_____

Who do we hear when we listen to Him?

_____

5. Pray silently: Each person think of a path reaching from you to God; realize again that path is Jesus. Thank Jesus for being your Way and allowing you to come to God in prayer in His name.

6. Read Romans 8:31–39

7. Discuss

a. When is it easy to believe God loves you?

b. When is it difficult to believe God loves you?

c. How important is it to your prayers that you believe God loves you?

8. Read Romans 8:15–16.

9. Discuss

a. What might be some of the differences in attitudes and feelings of security between a child who is shuffled between foster homes and one who is adopted into a loving family?

_____

_____

_____

b. How do the above differences apply to your adoption into God's family? Why is it important that you believe you are God's adopted daughter, God's child?

_____

_____

_____

c. How could knowing you are God's child affect your prayers?

_____

_____

_____

10. Share personal evidences of God's love—ways His love has made a difference in your life.

D. In groups of two to three people:

Share with each other an area of your life in which you need a stronger belief that God loves you. Pray for each other concerning this need.

3

THE RIGHT DIRECTION

It was a tall office building. Busy. Noisy. Indifferent. All around me people were pretending not to see each other.

As I started to board the elevator on the fourth floor, something stopped me. I stepped back out onto the fourth floor. Watching the elevator doors close, I wondered if the inner signal was really from God.

In the midst of the bustle of office personnel and clanging machines, God gave an inner quietness . . . and His guidance.

It's not always possible to bring the world around us to a screeching halt. Not even for a brief moment of prayer. Yet quietness is crucial for prayer. Quiet is as important for praying as the ignition key is for driving a car.

Psalm 46:10:

"Be still . . . " (King James).

"Stand silent . . . " (TLB).

"Pause a while . . . " (Jerusalem Bible).

"Cease striving . . ." (NASB).

We may not always be able to control the clamor or activity around us when we need to "be still," but I don't think that's what is meant by this Scripture.

It can be very quiet around us.

The radio off.

The telephone unplugged.

The house empty.

But inside . . .

inside we can still be frantically rushing around.

It's inside . . . inside that we *must* be still. Not in that critical moment where a quick prayer is required: as a child is darting onto a busy street, we don't pause and wait for an inner stillness before we cry out for God's protection. But, in our devotional times with our God, we must ask Him for an inner quiet . . . an inner stillness . . . if what follows is really to be *prayer*.

It's in that inner quiet

we find the *right direction* for our prayer.

In the late afternoon, as dusk slowly unfolds across the sky and the aroma of a cooking dinner circles to the ceiling, your family tumbles in the front door: "What's for dinner?" "Mom, did you wash my jeans?" "Honey, did you remember to go by the bank?"

Wouldn't it have been nice to have heard: "Hi, Mom, how are you doing?" "How was your day, Honey?"

It's easy to rush around doing what is important to *us* and not take note of those around us. We do the same thing with God. We come to our prayer time and rush into the "important" part: our requests. Often we take little notice of the One we're talking to. But that's more than a small oversight—it affects the direction of our entire prayer.

Direction makes a difference.

In conversation.

In life.

In prayer.

My parents, like so many "farm kids," have a built-in compass. That is not something I inherited. When I travel alone, I get lost with such consistency that service station attendants across the nation get out their maps when they see me drive in. In my attempt to arrive at my destination, I tend to waste time and gasoline because I lose my way.

It's possible to come to our prayer time sincerely and in need of help . . . to pour out our concerns to God . . . and to leave our prayer more upset than when we began. Or sometimes we finish our prayer no more relieved than had we confided our problem to an empty room.

The problem is

we were never *quiet* enough inside

to find the right direction for our prayer.

So we never reached our destination—God's help.

"Cease striving and know that I am God" (Ps. 46:10, NASB).

It sounds simple. Automatic. Obvious. But it isn't. Prayers are more often directed toward our *problems* or *ourselves* than God.

The right direction for our prayers is to look to God.

Only then does prayer make sense.

Only then does prayer work.

Only then do we feel like we've prayed.

LOOK AT GOD AND KNOW YOU ARE IN HIS PRESENCE

Otherwise we are talking to the air. Or ourselves.

We are in the Presence of our powerful and personal God. If you don't believe it, ask God to help you know it. If you don't feel it, ask Him to help you sense His Presence.

Sometimes you'll sense God right away. Sometimes you may not be sure He's even in heaven, let alone anywhere around you. In those days you need to spend more time . . .

Thinking about God.

Reflecting on your God.

Soon you will *know*

He is with you.

> "Acknowledge and take to heart this day that the Lord is God in heaven and on the earth below. There is no other" (Deut. 4:39).

LOOK TO GOD AND WORSHIP HIM

Acknowledge God as God, reaffirming your personal commitment to Jesus as Savior, to God as Lord. Think about the wonder of your God. Appreciate Him. Be filled with gratitude at the integrity of your God. Think . . . this powerful God is *yours*.

> *Worship* your God. Sing a song. Read a psalm. Remember what God has done in His Word. Remember what God has done for others. *Worship* your God.

Somehow such a focus picks us out of the quicksand and sticky traps of our problems and delivers us to a freer place . . . a place transformed by the perspective of a powerful God.

"Ascribe to the Lord the glory due His name; worship
the Lord in the splendor of His holiness." (Ps. 29:2).

LOOK AT GOD AND LEARN ABOUT HIM

We may think we know God. But often we know our
problems and our needs better than we know God. We may
spend so much time thinking about our needs—more time
than we think about God—that our picture of God becomes
hazy.

Learn about your God. Study Scriptures that describe
God. Study Jesus' life. Study Jesus' words. Study the
characteristics of God. Study the names given God in the
Bible. Learn about your God.

The better you know a friend, the more trustworthy you
discover her to be, the easier it is to confide in her—to trust
her counsel.

The better you know God, the easier it is to trust Him . . .
with your needs . . . with yourself . . . with the people you
love.

"Do you want more and more of God's kindness and
peace? Then learn to know Him better and better" (2 Pet.
1:2, TLB).

After standing a few minutes on the fourth floor, I sensed
God directing me to get back on the elevator. This time it was
empty. At the third floor one man got on. He looked like an
executive. Sixties. Graying. Glasses.

As we passed the second floor, I said, "You look troubled.
I want you to know, God really loves you and can help you.
I'll be praying for you this afternoon."

Startled, he turned to me. Tears welled up in his eyes as he
openly told me of his disillusionment with God as a young
man, and of his desperate need for help with a serious

problem. "I haven't allowed anyone to mention God in my presence for more than twenty years," he admitted.

In the lobby of a building I'd never been in before, this stranger and I talked. And we prayed. He accepted Jesus as his Savior.

In the midst of a clamoring place, God gave a quietness within, and helped me *look at Him.*

It was the right direction.

> "Look to the Lord and His strength; seek His face always" (1 Chron. 16:11).
>
> ". . . Then Jesus looked up and said, "Father . . . " (John 11:41).

PERSONAL DISCOVERIES IN PRAYER

1. Read Psalm 46:10.

   a. Ask God to help you discover the things that interfere with your focusing on Him. List them here.

   _____

   _____

   _____

   _____

   b. Pray separately for each item you've listed. Picture Jesus in front of you; think of yourself giving Him each of these items—one at a time—and leaving them in His hands; then consciously look from the interference to Jesus.

2. What is your most difficult time of the week?

   _____

   _____

    a. Think of Jesus in that scene.

    b. Ask God to help you sense Him in that situation.

    c. Thank Him that He is always with you even when you forget He's there.

3. Read Psalm 100:1–2. Tell God of your love for Him and why you love Him.

4. Read Psalm 100:3. Tell God how you feel about belonging to Him.

5. Read Psalm 100:4.

    a. Thank God for specific differences He has made in your life.

    b. Thank God for a difference He has made in the life of a loved one.

6. Read Psalm 100:5.

    a. Tell God of your favorite story in the Old Testament and why you like it. Tell God what you think it says about Him and how that makes you feel as His daughter.

    b. Tell God of your favorite story about Jesus in the Gospels and why it is your favorite. Tell God what you think it says about Him and how that makes you feel as His daughter.

    c. Tell God some of your favorite things about Him. Be specific.

7. Reread Psalm 100 *to God* as a prayer of praise from you.

SHARED DISCOVERIES IN PRAYER

A. As an entire group:

1. Read Psalm 121:1.

   "I will lift up my eyes to the hills—where does my help come from?"

2. Discuss

   a. When you pray, what might you focus on instead of God?

   _____

   _____

   _____

   b. Take each of the things just listed and discuss how focusing attention on it would affect your prayer time. (Make notes for personal review later.)

   _____

   _____

   _____

   _____

3. Read Psalm 121:2.

4. Discuss

   a. What question is answered in this verse?

   _____

   _____

   b. Would it have taken the psalmist longer to come to that answer had he not been looking to God with his original question? Why?

_____

_____

_____

B. In groups of five or six people:

1. Read Psalm 46:10. (If different translations are available, read from several.)

2. Memorize

   "Cease striving and know that I am God" (Ps. 46:10, NASB).

   a. Read the verse aloud in unison.

   b. Go around your circle, with each person saying one word of the verse until the verse has been completed and each person has said at least one word. (It may be necessary to say the verse several times in order to get around the circle.)

   c. Repeat "b" three times, each saying her word from memory. *Begin with a different person each time.*

   d. Say the verse again in unison from memory.

   e. Each who will, try to say the verse alone from memory.

   f. Say it in unison again.

3. Have each person share something that makes it difficult for her to "cease from striving" in her devotional times. After the first one shares, have the person to her left pray* for her. Then proceed on around the

_____

(*If a person wishes to, she may tell the group she'll lead in silent prayer—then do so.)

circle, with one sharing and the person to her left praying for her.

C. As an entire group:

1. Have everyone look up and one person read aloud Psalm 145:1–5.

2. Have a few share stories of God's help and greatness as told by their parents, older family members, friends, or from something they've read.

3. Have everyone follow as one person reads aloud Psalm 145:6–7.

4. Share

   a. A favorite story from the Bible that tells of God's power.

   b. A favorite story from the Bible that tells of God's goodness.

5. Discuss: Which of God's attributes does each of the following verses refer to? Why is it important for us to know God has that attribute? How should this knowledge affect our prayers?

   a. Psalm 145:9

   _____

   _____

   _____

   b. Psalm 145:13

   _____

   _____

   _____

c. Psalm 145:14

_____

_____

_____

d. Psalm 145:17

_____

_____

_____

e. Psalm 145:18

_____

_____

_____

6. Say the memory verse, Psalm 46:10, together again.

7. Discuss

a. When does singing become a prayer?

b. Select a song about God that could be a prayer of worship.

8. Pray

a. Sing a song about God as a prayer of worship.

b. Have each who wishes pray a sentence prayer aloud: Tell God something you like about Him.

c. Have one person close by praying aloud for the group: Ask God to teach each of you to look to Him in your prayers.

4

A UNIQUELY PERSONAL FRIENDSHIP

The Perfect Prayer Mold. Convinced it exists, we search for it. When we discover someone who seems to have found it, we're filled with questions: "How long do you pray"; "Where do you pray"; "What kind of prayer list do you use?" Surely when we stretch and squeeze ourselves into that person's mold, we'll produce an effective prayer life.

Learning from others can be helpful, but the call isn't to climb aboard a conveyor belt and be made over into clones of an ideal pray-er. We have instead an invitation to develop an intimate friendship with God.

> "Friendship with God is reserved for those who reverence Him. With them alone He shares the secrets of His promises" (Ps. 25:14, TLB).

If that fellowship—that prayer life—is to be what it can be, it must be *ours* . . . no one else's. It must fit *us*.

Jesus never asked Peter to be John or Zacchaeus to be Matthew. God doesn't command us to have a prayer time like anyone else. No, He longs for us to let Him develop a friendship with us that is uniquely ours. Oh, there'll be some stretching and molding as our prayer time develops, but we'll not be crowded into someone else's mold. We'll fit the pattern God cuts out just for us.

> "I will instruct you and teach you in the way you should go; I will counsel you and watch over you" (Ps. 32:8).

There are many levels of friendship: the friend we chat with casually; the friend we have serious talks with; the friend we confide in. Each of those ascending levels requires more work than the level preceding it.

We have the same possibilities with God. We can chat casually with Him; have serious talks; or commit ourselves to discover the intimacy of this friendship. We decide. *God's offer is for a uniquely personal friendship.*

> "I am the Lord your God, who brought you up out of Egypt. Open wide your mouth and I will fill it" (Ps. 81:10).

THE SCHEDULE IS PERSONAL

"I just can't! I try and I try, but I just can't stick with it. I know I have to if I'm going to grow in my relationship with my Lord." Karole's weary eyes and voice pleaded for help.

"I try to stay awake at night, but I always fall asleep while I'm praying. And mornings . . . well . . . I can't think in the morning. What can I do?" she asked me. "I really want to pray every day. I understand we're supposed to pray an hour, and it needs to be in the morning."

No complaints. No attempt to avoid the call to pray. And no reference to her schedule: ten hours a day of physical

) for her brain-damaged child. No
Three years of loving and taxing
, trying to have some emotional and
r husband and other children.

there is a magical time or perfect
" I said. "I don't think an hour is
ual than thirty minutes."

Karole said, slumping back in the
me, quieted by sleeping children,
husband looked as if he longed to

daughter," I continued. "No one
ou better than He does. Give God
e ever heard about. Allow Him the
devotional time that is uniquely
ur desire to spend time with Him.
than you do. He'll give you ideas."
d Jim.

*II Corinthians
13:11*

ck a certain exercise you do with
ch time you do that exercise you
omething," I explained. "Or an
u'll pray for others. Or during the
day or week, you might ask God to
u—to help you feel His love.

e one Scripture verse a week on a
to prop up in your son's therapy
God to teach you what that verse

es," encouraged Jim, "and the kids
rds. They'd love to help!"

"It never occurred to me to ask God to work out something
within my schedule," Karole whispered. "I thought I had to
do it like everyone else."

Then she looked up . . . relieved. I saw a sparkle in those tired eyes.

We are all so different. In personality. In strengths. In needs. In responsibilities. Many times within our lives our schedules and responsibilities change. We may care for infants, juggle job and family, send off our kids to school, attend to a developing career.

What we tend to do with our prayer time is give God the leftover moments—when we think of prayer at all. Or we relegate prayer to "quickie" pleas for help. God wants us to tell Him our needs, but I think He has more in mind for His friendship than an occasional "S.O.S."

Ask God to direct you in establishing realistic goals. Set goals small enough that you'll actually do them—not put them off. It's easy to set such big goals for yourself that you get discouraged before you even begin. God would rather have ten minutes each day with you than an hour you promise but never get around to. Then, *as you reach your goals, allow God to give you new goals.*

Let God Design Your Prayer Times.

> "Having started the ball rolling so enthusiastically, you should carry this project through to completion just as gladly. . . . Let your enthusiastic idea at the start be equalled by your realistic action now" (2 Cor. 8:11, TLB).

THE PLACE IS PERSONAL

Kneeling. Driving. A favorite room. A comfortable chair. You and God can work out where you usually have your prayer time. If it needs to be in your home, but it's difficult to keep your mind on God, pull a chair up to a window for your devotions.

Once in a while, have your devotions in a different place.

Ride your bike and talk with God. Sit in your backyard and talk with God. Pray in a different room, such as your child's bedroom. Go to your church for your personal quiet time.

> "For the eyes of the Lord are on the righteous and His ears are attentive to their cry" (Ps. 34:15).

THE TIME IS PERSONAL

When my brother's family visits, my nieces become my roommates. Four-year-old Cara wakes up with the sun, crawls in bed with me and whispers to me patiently while her older sister still sleeps. Christa, seven, wakes up only when she has no other choice. "I'm not a very good morning person," she told me one day as she struggled to wake up.

There is no perfect time for prayer that everyone must follow. Cara prays easily at dawn. It's best for Christa to wait until later in the day.

God will help you select a time for your devotions that is right for you. Remember not to give God leftover moments but allow Him the freedom to construct a prayer schedule that is best—one that will fit *you.*

The more you allow God to design your prayer times,
   the more you follow this design,
   the more that design will slowly be expanded.
      Until . . . eventually . . . a "night" person develops
      a desire to also greet God when she wakes up.

> "I will pray morning, noon, and night, pleading aloud with God; and He will hear and answer" (Ps. 55:17, TLB).

THE CONVERSATION IS PERSONAL

> "Don't worry about anything; instead, pray about everything; tell God your needs and don't forget to thank Him for His answers" (Phil. 4:6, TLB).

Philippians 4:6 tells us to talk to God about *anything*. We'd probably quickly agree. But, if encouraged to really talk to God about seemingly unimportant things, a lot of us feel awkward.

I wonder . . . if we worked on talking to God about *anything*, even the little things in life, if it wouldn't become easier to talk to God about the things we tend to keep hidden in our hearts. Then our friendship would be more comfortable, more complete.

You can have a running conversation with God throughout your day. You know, the thoughts that fill your days—you can tell them to God: "God, I don't know what to cook for dinner." "God, if this traffic doesn't let up, I'm going to be late for work." Talking to God throughout your day turns your thoughts to Him and makes it easier to remember to tell Him more important things.

You can tell God those feelings that erupt in your day. What we often do instead is wait until our feelings are so traumatized that we can no longer handle them . . . *then* we tell God. Wouldn't it be a healthier friendship if we'd share our feelings with God as they develop? If we'd get help with our problems at the beginning? "God, that hurt my feelings," or "God, I can't figure out why I feel so sad."

Talking with God throughout our day is an important part of our friendship, but it's not enough. We can't limit our conversation to talking on the run if the friendship is to become intimate. That set apart time—that quiet time with God—is still important.

We tend to tell God what we think we should. No wonder our prayer time is so often meaningless! When David the psalmist felt deserted, he didn't say, "Oh, God, I know You are here and love me." No, he prayed, "My God, my God, why have you forsaken me?" (Ps. 22:1).

We don't have to protect God from our struggles. How is He to help us if we don't open our hearts to Him?

"God, I don't want to pray. I'm sorry; please help me."

"God, I just don't believe You care. Please help me."

"God, why aren't You doing something about this?"

"God, I'm not sure You are powerful enough to help. Forgive me. Help me to trust You."

Whatever your struggle . . . you can present it to God. Honestly tell God where your heart is and then stay in your prayer time long enough to receive God's help. His love for you frees you to be honest in your conversation with Him.

"He will call upon me, and I will answer him; I will be with him in trouble, I will deliver him and honor him" (Ps. 91:15).

THE PROCESS IS PERSONAL

As you pursue intimacy with God, He leads you in paths that ensure closer unity with Him. One path that clears away activities and releases God's power is fasting.

Fasting—going without something, usually food—is one way of saying to God: This is very important! Important enough for extra effort on my part.

In Daniel's partial fast, he ate only fruit and vegetables (Dan. 10:2–3). God will personalize your fast to fit you. Work out with Him if you are to fast a portion of a meal, a complete meal, a series of meals, or if you are to give up something other than food.

When a burden is aching within you and you long to *do* something, respond to God's call to fast (Isa. 58:6–9). Willingly accept His guidance to fast whenever a particular prayer requires it. Eventually, you may feel led to fast as a regular part of your prayer life.

Fasting releases God's power, clears vision, enhances discernment, reveals God's will. It's a sacred offer of closeness from our God.

> "So we fasted and petitioned our God about this, and he answered our prayer" (Ezra 8:23).

THE CALL IS PERSONAL

You can't become friends with someone without spending time with him, whether that time is on the phone, through letters, or in person. You can learn about someone, care about someone, even feel as though you know someone without ever meeting him. But you can't become friends with someone unless you spend time with him.

You can *learn* about God without spending time with Him. You can *care* for God without spending time with Him. You can *feel* you know God without spending time with Him. But the only way to develop your friendship with God is to spend time with Him.

We decide, you and I, what kind of friendship we have with God. We determine if that friendship is to grow in intimacy or if we are going to settle for the present level.

There's more.

There's always more. More intimacy. More fellowship. More understanding. More vision.

That's one of the exciting things about belonging to God. No matter how much we learn, how close we are to God . . . there's more.

We decide, you and I. God's call is to us, personally.

> "But as for me, I get as close to Him as I can!" (Ps. 73:28, TLB).

PERSONAL DISCOVERIES IN PRAYER

1. Read Romans 11:33.

    a. Thank God for His wisdom and power.

    b. Ask God to share that wisdom with you as you complete this devotional.

2. Read Romans 11:36.

    a. Thank God for two things happening in your life.

    b. Thank God for something He has done for two other people.

    c. Talk with God about the kind or depth of friendship you have with Him.

3. Read Romans 12:2.

    a. Give to God all your preconceived ideas about prayer and ask Him to help you develop your own personal fellowship with Him.

    b. Talk with God about your schedule. Don't just think it through on your own, but decide with God the best time to have your devotions. Write that decision here:

_____

    c. Talk with God about the best place for you to have your devotions. Write your decision here:

_____

_____

    d. Talk with God about how often you will have a set quiet time—beginning now. Allow God to help you set realistic goals, and as you reach those goals, allow God to increase them. Write your decision here:

_____

_____

4. Read Romans 12:12.

   a. Talk with God honestly about your joy: its abundance or absence or inconsistency. Ask His help.

   b. Allow God to bring to your mind some needs that you had previously thought were too insignificant to present to Him. Talk with Him now about them.

   c. Talk with God about your deepest needs. Honestly tell Him the kind of help you need and any discouragement, anger, or confusion you are experiencing concerning His answer to your prayers. Allow God to guide your thoughts. Ask Him to help you.

   d. Thank God for wanting you to give your needs to Him.

   e. Ask God to teach you what Isaiah 58:6–9 has to say to you concerning your prayer life.

5. Read Romans 12:13. Ask God to bring one person to your mind who needs help. Pray for that person.

SHARED DISCOVERIES IN PRAYER

A. As an entire group:

1. Read John 15:15.

2. Discuss

   a. What do you look for in a good friend?

   _____

   _____

   b. What are the differences between a casual friendship and a close friendship?

   _____

_____

_____

c. How do you become close friends with someone?

_____

_____

3. Read John 15:15 again.

4. Discuss

    a. Why does Jesus call us friends?

_____

    b. What would be the differences in a casual friendship with God and a close, intimate friendship with God? (In both situations the person is a Christian.)

_____

_____

    c. How would praying differ in these two relationships?

_____

    d. How do we become close friends with God?

_____

5. Read Philippians 4:6 in unison.

"Don't worry about anything; instead, pray about everything; tell God your needs and don't forget to thank Him for His answers" (TLB).

6. Discuss

    a. What does this verse say we should talk to God about?

_____

b. What is easy for you to talk to God about? (This may be different with each individual.)

c. What is difficult for you to talk to God about? (This also differs with people.)

d. What would make it easier to talk to God about difficult things?

_____

_____

B. In groups of four or five people:

1. Tell about one of your good friends; how you met, why this person is such a good friend, and how you developed that friendship.

2. Pray around your circle for each item listed below before you move on to the next item. (If at any time you prefer not to pray aloud when it's your turn, touch the arm of the person next to you. She'll then pray aloud.)

    a. Tell God what your favorite day of the week is and why.

    b. Tell God what your worst day of the week is and why.

    c. Tell God what your favorite color is and why.

    d. Ask God's help for some small project you are working on.

    e. Tell God you love Him.

    f. After each shares a serious need, the one on her left pray* aloud for that need.

---

*If it's your turn to pray and you prefer not to pray aloud, tell the group you'll lead in silent prayer.

C. As an entire group:

1. Read Psalm 22:1–3.

   a. Why is David able to be so honest with God?

   _____

   b. Why is such total honesty with God important?

   _____

   c. What keeps us from being honest with God?

   _____

   _____

   _____

   d. What relationship would these verses have to David's ability to *honestly* pray Psalm 23:1–2?

   _____

2. Have each person pray silently: Ask God's help in being honest with Him; present to God any area of your life in which you have a problem being open with Him.

3. Share with the group your discoveries this last week about your personal friendship with God and your personal prayer times.

4. Read Psalm 25:14 in unison.

   "Friendship with God is reserved for those who reverence Him. With them alone He shares the secrets of His promises" (TLB).

5. Have those who wish to, pray aloud. Tell God the kind of friendship they want to have with Him.

5

WHAT DO YOU HEAR?

You need direction to a specific address:

You stop the car, tell someone where you are going, and ask how to get there . . .

. . . But before he answers, you roll your car window up, drive away, and look for the address.

You want to know the ingredients in a friend's favorite recipe:

You call the friend, tell her how much you love her salad, and ask for the recipe . . .

. . . Then you hang up before she answers and try to figure out how to make the salad.

You need some facts from a colleague at work before you can complete your project:

You walk over to his desk, tell him what you need . . .

. . . Then turn and walk back to your desk to finish your project without the needed information.

Absurd reactions? We'd never do that?

Not to anyone but God.

Whether we casually or desperately tell God our needs, we rarely wait to hear what God has to say. We listen more readily to a friend, a minister, a counselor—even a stranger—than we listen to God.

We learn so much by what we hear: a clamoring bell tells us to answer the phone; the clanking in a car tells us it needs work; a child's laughter tells us he likes our teasing. If we have a hearing impairment, we learn to "listen" with our eyes, with our hearts. Whatever our method, we learn by what we hear.

People often tell me, "God never speaks to me." I don't believe it. I think, instead, it's a matter of not "hearing" Him.

We aren't going to receive a telegram signed "The Almighty." God won't interrupt our television program with a special bulletin to us. But if we have accepted Jesus as our Savior, then we are in a position to hear God.

Sometimes God speaks to us through trusted Christians. Sometimes He speaks to us through circumstances. God sometimes speaks to us in our thoughts.

But all of those methods are meant to supplement God speaking to us through His Word—the Bible. But before we can consistently hear God through His Word, we have to believe He *will* talk to us!

WHAT DO YOU HEAR when you have a problem?

Your anxieties? Your fears? Your own solutions?

WHAT DO YOU HEAR when you need direction?

Advice from a wise person? Thoughts of a popular author? Your own confusion?

WHAT DO YOU HEAR when you feel alone?

The emptiness? The darkness? The comfort of a friend?

WHAT DO YOU HEAR when you need a vision?

The pulse of those around you? Old fantasies? New hopes?

WHAT DO YOU HEAR when there is nothing to do?

Television? Radio? Your mental wanderings?

In the eighth grade I decided I'd never be a teacher. Approaching my last year of college, God directed I was to teach. Pacified somewhat by the sense that it would only be for a few years, I scrambled to change my classes and to get a teaching credential.

Since I knew I had to teach, I decided what kind of teaching position I'd enjoy and went looking. Halfway into that first year of teaching—with things going well—God showed me that *I* had selected the school, not He. I'd heard His direction to teach, then went off to do it without waiting for further guidance.

I had never realized before that—even with my sincere desire for God to be in charge of my life—I had heard my own desires more than I had heard what God wanted.

I asked God to teach me to hear *HIM*.

As the weeks passed, I increasingly felt there was a specific school where God wanted me, so I resigned and went looking. Each time I was offered a job, I prayed and heard God say no.

One day, as I was applying for a job, the personnel

director offered me a completely different assignment. It was one of those instances when I didn't *need* to ask God—I knew right away I didn't want it! I answered with a quick no.

In the middle of that night, I couldn't sleep and began to pray. Immediately I realized God was displeased with me about something . . . I'd turned down the job He had been saving for me. I couldn't believe it! It was junior high; I loved high school. They were subjects I'd never taught before, in a community where violence and drugs made any kind of true teaching difficult.

I finally said a reluctant okay and went to sleep. I hoped it was one of those instances that you hear about when God wants a person to say yes, but only means it as a test of faith—not as something you really have to do.

The next morning another struggle with God ended with my call to the personnel director. What ultimately followed was a great privilege: Three years of teaching unbathed, emotionally scarred, physically abused twelve- and thirteen-year-olds. More and more God opened opportunities to share Christ with them, and when I resigned, God had given me the privilege of praying with more than one thousand students, some for their deep needs, or for salvation.

I would have missed so much had I only "heard" myself. Besides having the opportunity to share Jesus with kids who knew nothing about Him, God was planting seeds in my own life: a beginning growing awareness of God's ability to guide me in the face of my ignorance and awareness of my need to depend on Him. God built on the lessons of those years when He developed my personal prayer ministry.

> "Trust in the Lord with all your heart and *lean not on your own understanding;* in *all* your ways acknowledge Him, and He will make your paths straight" (Prov. 3:5–6, emphasis mine).

WE NEED TO HEAR **God's desire to talk to us.**

God wants to talk to us. It's inherent in His nature. God wants to talk to *us*. It's inherent in our adoption.

It comes with the relationship.

God doesn't comb the world looking for a select few to communicate with. He waits for His children to hear Him.

According to his own assessment, Moses wasn't a good speaker. Evidently God hadn't searched out a great orator. He had searched out someone who would listen to and follow His instructions. Moses didn't just respond to the fire of the burning bush—he heard God.

If you don't believe God wants to consistently talk to you, then that's where you begin: "God, please teach me You *want* to talk to *me*."

> "Call unto me and I will answer you and tell you great
> and unsearchable things you do not know" (Jer. 33:3).

WE NEED TO HEAR GOD **to understand His will.**

With the passage of time and the influence of our humanness, praying for God's will has eroded into something we say but don't mean. Or our belief in God's sovereignty is reflected in a statement of giving up, "Oh, well, He's going to do what He wants anyway." Or we grit our teeth and clench our fists . . . steeling ourselves to accept God's distasteful will.

Here is God . . . all powerful . . . all wise . . . all loving . . . and we act as if whatever He wants for us would be the worst thing that could ever happen. Oh, we don't usually admit it to each other . . . but listen to our conversations. Do we consider God's will exciting, adventuresome, fulfilling? Something to be actively, joyously sought? Or worse than taking castor oil?

Think of it! Whatever we present to God, He actually has a

will for it, a plan for it. His is a will we can *trust*. It's a will that ensures us of fulfillment. It's a will that fulfills God's purposes through us.

Even with a healing of our attitude and our response to God's will, there may still be times of struggle against His will. But those times become fewer and less difficult if we'll spend time hearing God. The more we hear Him, the more we know we don't have to be afraid of His will.

> "Not everyone who says to Me, 'Lord, Lord,' will enter the kingdom of heaven, but only he who does the will of My Father who is in heaven" (Matt. 7:21).

> " 'For I know the plans I have for you,' declares the Lord, 'plans to prosper you and not to harm you, plans to give you hope and a future' " (Jer. 29:11).

WE NEED TO HEAR GOD **to have a growing faith.**

We tend to be so self-absorbed that we accept the responsibility of orchestrating everything, even our faith. Faith isn't something you work up. Faith isn't figuring out what you want and then taking extra vitamin pills so you can be especially determined to receive it. Faith isn't goose bumps, followed by sincere attempts to make that feeling linger until we receive the help we need.

Faith is God's gift of belief—belief that God is going to do what He said. So we have to hear what He says before we can have faith.

Sarah didn't walk up to Abraham one day and say, "Abe, I'm so bored! I've figured out what I can do to make my life more interesting—I've decided to have a baby."

"What!" Abraham might have responded in disbelief. "Woman, you're old! This spring day has gone to your head, or you're so old it's affecting your mind!"

"No," Sarah might have insisted, "I've decided. This is

what I want, and I'm just going to believe with all my might. I'll work up enough faith to believe it's going to happen, and I know if I do, that God will do it for me.''

That wasn't Sarah's or Abraham's reaction—although it may be fairly close to how *we* might have responded. But then—it wouldn't have been faith. Not the kind God talks about. ''By faith Abraham, even though he was past age—and Sarah herself was barren—was enabled to become a father because he considered Him faithful who had made the promise'' (Heb. 11:11).

Even if we believe God's call for stable, consistent faith (Heb. 11:1), we often dutifully try to produce it. We don't realize we need to first hear what God wants us to believe, what He wants us to have faith for. First comes the hearing, then follows the faith. If the faith doesn't come, then that's where we pray:

> ''God, I believe You said this. But I'm sorry
> I don't believe You'll do it. Please give me
> faith in *You*. In what You have directed.''

But . . . the hearing comes first!

> ''Let us fix our eyes on Jesus the author and perfector of our faith'' (Heb. 12:2a).

WE NEED TO HEAR GOD because we need HIM!

If we're really honest, we'll admit there are a lot of times we don't believe we need God. Oh, in times of crisis of course we know we need God. But in the moments of our daily lives there are a lot of things we can accomplish with little attention to God.

God's wondrous love offers you the privilege of growing and maturing in your friendship with Him. But you have to remember: You never grow up! You remain God's child. God made no provision for you to come to Him as a peer, only as His child—that vulnerable, dependent relationship of daughter to Father.

You have to believe it! If you don't, pray:

"God, part of me knows it, but most of me forgets it. Show me my need to depend on You . . . to hear You."

Hearing God is an investment. Of time. Of energy. Of focus. Of inner stillness. To pay that price, we have to believe we *need* to hear God.

But . . .

the investment becomes nothing compared to hearing God.

"He replied, 'Blessed rather are those who hear the word of God and obey it' " (Luke 11:28).

PERSONAL DISCOVERIES IN PRAYER

1. Read Psalm 119:18–19.

   a. What percentage of your prayer time are *you* the one who is talking?

   _____

   b. What importance do you give to *listening* to God in your prayer time?

   _____

   c. Talk to God about any problems you have with listening to Him. Ask for His help.

2. Read Psalm 119:20.

   a. Ask God to help you *want* to hear what He has to say to you.

   b. Ask God to help you know you *need* to hear what He has to say to you.

3. Read Psalm 119:25.

   a. When you have a problem, to whom do you go and/or what do you usually do first for help?

   _____

   _____

   _____

   b. Ask God to help you trust Him more completely and more quickly.

4. Read Psalm 119:26. Ask God to help you listen to Him after you ask for His help.

5. Read Psalm 119:105. Ask God to help you believe that He *will* talk with you through His Word.

6. Read Psalm 119:114.

   a. Talk to God about your feelings and beliefs concerning this verse.

   b. Ask God to help you believe this verse and act on that belief more than you ever have before.

7. Read Psalm 119:140.

   a. Reflect on times when God has guided you and helped you. Thank Him for talking to you in those times.

   b. Reflect on times when God has specifically talked to others and thank Him for that.

8. Read Psalm 119:160,165.

   a. Ask God to give you a great love for His Word.

   b. Ask God to teach you to listen to Him.

SHARED DISCOVERIES IN PRAYER

A. As an entire group:

"He who has ears to hear, let him hear" (Luke 14:35b).

1. Read John 10:4.

    a. Whose voices do you recognize on the phone after a sentence or two? After only hearing a single word?

    b. How do you come to recognize a voice quickly?

    _____

    c. How would recognizing voices over the phone apply to recognizing God's voice?

    _____

    _____

2. Read John 10:27.

    a. According to this verse, whose voice do God's followers listen to?

    _____

    b. To whom do you usually go to if you have a problem?

    _____

    c. To whom do you tell good and exciting news?

    _____

    d. What makes someone a trusted counselor?

    _____

    _____

    e. Why is it easier to listen to people than to God?

    _____

    _____

   f. Reread John 10:27. In what ways are the three parts
      of this verse dependent on each other?

   _____

   _____

3. Have each woman pray silently: Ask God to help you
   want to hear Him; ask God to teach you to know His
   voice.

4. Why do the following Scriptures say we should listen to
   God? In each instance, discuss: What are some practical contributions listening would make to your prayer
   life; do you have a personal experience with this kind of
   guidance?

   a. Matthew 7:24

   _____

   _____

   b. Isaiah 30:21

   _____

   _____

   c. John 14:26

   _____

   _____

5. Have one person pray aloud for the group, asking God
   to teach each of you to listen to Him.

6. What part does spending enough time with God to
   listen to Him play in the following Scriptures?

   a. John 5:9

   _____

   _____

b. John 6:38

_____

_____

c. Psalm 40:8

_____

_____

7. Have those who desire, share a time that they heard God's will. What difference did it make in their attitudes or actions?

8. Read the following in unison.

"This is the assurance we have in approaching God: that if we ask anything according to His will, He hears us. . . . Consequently, faith comes from hearing the message, and the message is heard through the word of Christ. . . . 'Have faith in God,' Jesus answered" (1 John 5:14; Rom. 10:17; Mark 11:22).

B. In groups of two to five people:

Pray aloud for each other as each shares:

1. A specific situation or problem in which she needs to hear God's voice.

2. An area in which she has heard God's voice but needs a stronger faith to believe Him.

6

LISTEN ... GOD IS TALKING

It doesn't happen in a moment. You don't take an infant just beginning to understand words and strap him to a chair in a college lecture room. A lot of learning takes place between those two points. It takes time.

We want God to tell us His grand plan. Some secret insight . . . a continual string of personal revelations. But it doesn't happen in a moment. Learning to listen to God is a process. It takes time. Time in God's Word.

Jesus said we'd know His voice (John 10:4). Just as a tiny baby recognizes the voices of those he spends the most time with, so the more time we spend listening to God the more easily we recognize His voice.

God's voice is always consistent with His character.

This is reason why we need to become well acquainted with Him. To better understand His love, His purity, His

t us to do or say or think anything
onoring to Him. He'll never tell us
nt with Him.

onsistent with the spirit of the

can be pulled and twisted to prove
at you feel God is saying to you
irit of God's Word?

time to make sure it is God

re. We need to be careful not to set
as signs of His guidance. But if you
doing something you aren't sure is
n't from Him. God gives you time to
d it's His voice.

t believe every spirit, but test the
they are from God, because many
one out into the world'' (1 John

er peace.

s unsettling, scarey . . . there is deep
explain. If the peace isn't there, we
can ask God for His peace as His witness that this is *His*
voice.

"You will keep in perfect peace him whose mind is
steadfast, because he trusts in you" (Isa. 26:3).

God's voice is heard in His Word.

God's voice can often be verified by trusted Christians and circumstances. But not always. Sometimes His message is too personal, and He has not shared it with others.

Although others can often give us wonderful and needed encouragement, we shouldn't lean on them. And when we do go to someone for guidance, we should allow God to direct us to *His* person for that need, that time. We need to learn to listen—learn to recognize God's voice to *us*.

The most valid way God talks to us is His Spirit interpreting His Word—the Bible—to us.

The Bible is more than words.

It is more than Holy Words.

It is more than God's Holy Words.

The Bible is God's personal message to *you*.

If you don't believe that, pray:

"God, please help me to believe this book is Your message to *me*.

Don't read the Bible on your own. Always ask the Holy Spirit to help you understand what this passage has to say to you on this day.

"Your words are a flashlight to light the path ahead of me, and keep me from stumbling" (Ps. 119:105, TLB).

BE PREPARED FOR THE INTERRUPTERS:

... If your mind wanders: Write down your thought—"Buy milk," "Meeting tomorrow at 2," etc. Writing down the interrupters frees your thoughts to go back to prayer.

... If you catch yourself doing all the talking: Stop. Back up. Think about God, and ask Him to help you believe you *need* to listen to Him.

... If your thoughts are hurried and you can't slow them down: Walk to a window and look at nature, or stand

and gently shake yourself as you ask God to free your thoughts so you can listen.

If you're not accustomed to reading the Bible, begin with a short book. Mark is the shortest Gospel. Galatians, Ephesians, Philippians, Colossians each have just a few chapters. Knowing your book is short may help you finish it.

Set a realistic goal. God would rather you listen to three verses a day than to promise to read a chapter you never have time for. The next time, pick up where you left off until you complete your book (unless God directs otherwise).

Each time you are ready for a new book in the Bible, allow God to guide in which book to read. You may not always sense some special leading, but allow God the opportunity to direct. More and more you will know which book is right to read next. God knows what He wants to say to you, so He knows which book would most meet your needs.

You may sometimes hear people talk about praying and reading the Bible. If reading your Bible is more than just reading, if it is truly *listening,* then it is a crucial part of prayer—not separated from it.

The more your prayer life develops, the less time you will spend talking. The more time you will spend listening.

God has much to say to *you.* About Himself. About you. About His mission for you.

Listen.

God is talking.

"All who listen to my instructions and follow them are wise, like a man who builds his house on solid rock" (Matt. 7:24 ,TLB).

PERSONAL DISCOVERIES IN PRAYER

(This devotional may take several days to complete. Don't rush yourself to finish.)

1. Read 2 Timothy 3:16–17.

   a. Rewrite this Scripture, inserting your name often as if God is speaking directly to you.

      All scripture is God breathed and is useful for teaching Diane rebuking, correcting and training her her in righteousness so that Diane may be thoroughly equipped for every good work.

   b. Ask God to help you believe the Bible is His personal message to you.

   c. The Bible is God's personal message to me,

      _____.
      (write in your name)

2. Read Isaiah 48:12–13. Listen to this Scripture: What does it tell you about your God?

   He is expressing his thoughts in a personal way. He is telling of his greatness as Creator.

3. Read Proverbs 11:20b and Isaiah 50:4–5. Listen to these Scriptures by:

   a. Allowing God to remind you of a time when you helped someone. Think about how that pleases Him.

b. Allowing God to remind you of a time you listened and obeyed Him. Think about how that pleases Him.

4. Read Isaiah 51:3. Listen.

   a. Is there some area of your life in which you need God's comfort? Ask for and receive that comfort now.

   b. Do you know someone who needs comforting? Pray for that person now.

5. Read Isaiah 52:1–2. Listen.

   Ask God if there is an area of your life in which you need God's strength. Let God begin to strengthen you now.

6. Read Isaiah 55:1–2. Listen.

   Are you needy? Ask for and receive God's help. Be specific.

7. Read Isaiah 55:8–9. Listen.

   Ask God if He wants to say anything to you concerning any of your plans or responsibilities.

8. Read Isaiah 59:1–2. Listen.

   Is there anything for which you need to ask God's forgiveness? Listen to His Spirit and take care of that now.

9. Read Psalm 63:7. Listen.

   Are there things you've never praised God for or haven't thought of in a long time? Praise Him now.

SHARED DISCOVERIES IN PRAYER - *Read II Tim 3:10-17*

A. As an entire group:

1. Read 2 Timothy 3:16–17.

2. What are the purposes of God's Word listed in this Scripture?

3. Have different people share favorite Scripture passages and how God has used them in their lives.

    Phil 4:6-7

4. Have each person select one of the following topics to listen to what God has to say: wisdom, comfort, self-concept, fear.

5. Form small groups around each topic.

    a. If three to six people prefer a topic not listed, and concordances are available, form a group around that topic.

    b. Each topic listed doesn't need to be covered—just those of interest.

    c. All those who selected the same topic should group together. If a group is larger than six people, divide into smaller groups.

B. As small groups:

1. Have each person share the importance the Bible had in her home as she grew up.

2. Have each person who wishes to, pray aloud, telling God how she *wants* to feel about His Word.

3. Have each person silently ask God to speak to her as she listens to what He says about the topic.

4. Look up the Scriptures listed for your topic under #5 and any other Scriptures you know of relating to the topic. If you have a concordance, you might use it to look up additional verses.

a. Select meaningful Scriptures to make notes of, and rewrite them inserting your names, your needs, etc. (You can all read the Scriptures together, or divide them among your group until the final selection.)

b. As a group, work from your notes and form all the Scriptures into a letter from God to each of you.

c. Select someone to read your letter to the whole group at the end of this session.

5. Suggested topics:

Wisdom: Psalm 51:6; 111:10; Proverbs 1:5; 2:1–6; 3:5–8, 13–18; 4:5–6; 7:2–4; 8:1–7; 9:9; 11:12; Jeremiah 9:23–24; Matthew 7:24; Mark 12:32–34; James 1:5; 3:13, 17.

Comfort: Psalm 18:6; 31:7a; 40:11; 63:6–8; 103:4; 107:13–15; 119:114; Isaiah 40:1–2, 27–29; 41:10–13; 51:12; 61:3; John 14:15, 18; 2 Corinthians 1:3–4.

Self Concept: Psalm 8:4–6; 139; Isaiah 43:1–3; 45:9–10; 46:3–4; Jeremiah 18:2–6; John 15:3–5, 8–9; Ephesians 2:10.

Fear: Psalm 4:8; 18:1–3; 23; 91:1–6; 94:18–19; 125:1–2; Isaiah 41:10, 13–14; 43:1–3; Lamentations 3:55–58; John 3:16–18; 12:46; 14:27; 1 John 4:18.

C. As an entire group:

1. Ask a representative of each group to read her group's letter from God. Everyone should listen and let God talk to her through the letters.

2. Share

   a. Your feelings as you worked on your letter.

   b. What you learned from listening to these Scriptures.

   c. Anything special God has taught you in the last couple of weeks about hearing Him.

3. Have everyone who feels led pray aloud: Thank God for talking to you and mention specific times He's talked to you.

7

PRAYER'S NOURISHMENT

The shopping center bustled with fall's back-to-school shopping. I saw a woman crumpled over on a bench with her head in her hands. Even though I was too far away to see her clearly, I could feel her deep sadness. I sensed God wanted me to go sit by her and let Him open an opportunity to minister. But . . . it was late . . . and I was busy . . . although I paused . . . I walked on.

When I got to the door to leave the mall, I looked back. She was still in the same position. I hurriedly told myself it was *my* impression to talk to her and not God's leading.

We want to live our lives in isolated, separate packages. We don't want to think of our lives as interconnected. But they are! We *really* think when it's an important matter of obedience that we'll come through for God . . . but lesser things don't matter that much. Or, when we do obey, we want to be handed an abundant reward. Probably, most of all, *we don't want to have to obey.*

God told Moses to throw down his stick, and it became a snake. God told Moses to pick up the snake, and it became a stick again. What Moses saw during that process was critical for his belief in God's mission for him. But what if Moses had not dropped the stick? It was such a small and seemingly unimportant act. But what would the repercussions of disobedience have been? Is it even possible that Moses might not have possessed the faith to tell the people God's message? (Exod. 4.)

We want to think *our* disobedience isn't important . . . or is something we can make up for later.

In the mall's parking lot, I sat in my car, heavy with the weight of disobedience. Finally, I went back into the mall and walked toward the bench . . . but she was gone. I looked around but didn't know whom to look for because I hadn't bothered to get close enough to her to see what she looked like. My heart cried out to God, "Please, forgive me. You gave the opportunity of ministering, of helping someone in need, and I threw it away."

Walking back to my car, I prayed for the stranger. I asked God to bring someone across her path who would be more obedient than I was.

Prayer isn't a bottled moment in our day.
Our lives have to back up our prayers.
Our obedience nourishes our prayer time.

"But Jesus told him, '. . . the Scriptures tell us that bread won't feed men's souls: obedience to every word of God is what we need'" (Matt. 4:4, TLB).

As a child's muscles become stronger when he moves from crawling to walking to running, so our ability to hear God's voice becomes stronger as we act on what we hear.

In your prayer time, ask God for direction concerning what He wants you to do. Listen. Hear what He has to say. Then do what He tells you to!

Follow through on those thoughts to call a friend, write an encouraging note, let someone know you care.

As we follow these small directions, God trusts us with more. Why should He give us further guidance when we aren't acting on what He's already shown us? If we aren't trustworthy with a small assignment, why should He entrust something more to us?

> "His master replied, 'Well done, good and faithful servant! You have been faithful with a few things; I will put you in charge of many things. Come and share your master's happiness!' " (Matt. 25:21).

> "Jesus replied, 'If anyone loves me, he will obey my teaching' " (John 14:23).

It's not a single obedience. We're not to obey once and then stand around and wait for our dreams to come true. You don't plant one seed in your flower garden and then watch each day to see if it has become a bed of flowers.

No, we must build obedience upon obedience.

It's a lifestyle.

It's an active decision.

It's a continuing commitment:

TO OBEY GOD.

Prayer is not just the quiet moments with God. True prayer extends into our lives. The two of them—our prayer times and our lives—need to be consistent with each other for God's power to be freely released in our prayers.

Obedience is the nourishment for our prayers. It's the life-giving food that makes our prayer times powerful.

> "If you obey My commands, you will remain in My love, just as I have obeyed My Father's commands and remain in His love" (John 15:10).

PERSONAL DISCOVERIES IN PRAYER

(You may find the Table of Contents at the front of your Bible helpful. It lists the page numbers of the different books.)

1. Ask God to speak through these following Scriptures on obedience—to personalize them for you.

2. Genesis 4:6–7. What will happen if you don't obey God?

3. Genesis 6:8–10, 22.

   a. Why was Noah a delight to God?

   _____

   _____

   b. Think of a time when you obeyed God. Think of how you felt knowing you had obeyed. According to these verses, write out God's response to your obedience, inserting your name.

   _____

   _____

4. Matthew 4:4. What does Jesus say we need?

   _____

   _____

5. Ask God to help you believe in the importance of your own personal obedience.

6. Rewrite Matthew 4:4 as if Jesus is talking to you, inserting your name.

   _____

   _____

   _____

7. Luke 8:21. What do you have to do for Jesus to consider you as part of His family?

   _____

8. Acts 5:29. You are to obey God, not _____

9. Talk to God about your feelings concerning obedience. Ask God for the desire to obey Him.

10. Philippians 2:13. Who will help you obey God? _____

11. Ask God for the strength to obey Him.

12. Hebrews 5:8. Who learned obedience here? _____

13. Ask the Holy Spirit to reveal some specific ways in which you are to be obedient. List them here. Allow God to talk to you about them. Make some specific commitments.

   _____

   _____

   _____

   _____

14. Thank God that His every request for your obedience is valid. Thank Him that He will help you obey.

15. Think of the obedience of one other person that has directly benefited your life. Thank God for that person's obedience.

SHARED DISCOVERIES IN PRAYER

A. As an entire group:

1. Read Psalm 40:8 in unison.

   "And I delight to do Your will, my God, for your law is written upon my heart!" (TLB).

2. Discuss

   a. The difference in how you feel when a child happily obeys, obeys with resignation, obeys but gripes, doesn't obey.

   _____

   _____

   _____

   _____

   b. What is the difference each of those reactions makes in the child?

   _____

   _____

   _____

   _____

   c. How could these things apply to our response to disobeying to God?

   _____

   _____

   _____

   d. How could we learn to "delight" to do God's will?

   _____

   _____

B. In groups of two or three people:

1. Read Luke 11:28.

2. Share with each other any help you feel you need with the concept of obeying God, or a specific matter of obedience you need help with. Pray for each other.

C. As an entire group, look at God's instructions in the following Scriptures. These are instructions concerning our conversation that we are to obey.

1. Have everyone look up and one person read aloud Matthew 12:33–37.

2. Have everyone silently reread verses 36 and 37, inserting her name for "you" and "man."

'3. Discuss:
   Do we live as though we believe this Scripture? Why?

4. For each of the following Scriptures, discuss:

   a. Examples of obeying and disobeying God's instructions. (These can be real situations or hypothetical examples for the purpose of discussion.)

   b. How does this obedience or disobedience affect us?

   c. How does this obedience or disobedience affect others?

   d. How does this obedience or disobedience affect God and His purpose?

   Proverbs 11:13

   a. example: _____

   b. affect us: _____

   c. affect others: _____

d. affect God, His purpose: _____

Proverbs 26:20

a. example: _____

b. affect us: _____

c. affect others: _____

d. affect God, His purpose: _____

Proverbs 12:25

a. example: _____

b. affect us: _____

c. affect others: _____

d. affect God, His purpose: _____

1. Thessalonians 5:11

a. example: _____

b. affect us: _____

c. affect others: _____

d. affect God, His purpose: _____

5. Have everyone pray silently. Allow God to talk to each of you about your conversation.

6. Those who wish, share an instance when another person's obedience to God contributed to your life.

7. Have one person close in prayer, praying Psalm 143:10 as part of that prayer.

8

A LOVE GIFT

Several hundred college students crowded into our Sunday school room for my farewell party. I was leaving my job as my church's college director, and I'd miss this class of eager college kids.

Their presents were generous; their book of letters encouraging; the thoughts they expressed affirming. But the love gift which spoke the loudest was a scroll:

> "In support of God's call to a life of prayer, each of us will be praying and fasting for you one meal a week for the next two weeks. We will be asking God to release His power in your new ministry."
>
> A long list of names followed.

Praying for someone is a tremendous investment, and I felt indebted to them for so willingly investing in God's call to me. I knew their prayers would make a difference.

I was also thrilled for *them*. I thanked God that they knew so early in their lives what a loving gift prayer is.

GOD TELLS US TO PRAY FOR OTHERS

How selfish we'd be to hoard the benefits of fellowship with God. God doesn't give us a treasured friendship only to help *us*. Through prayer, He gives us the privilege of ministry to others. There's no understanding why He so honors us, but He does.

"... Pray much for others; plead for God's mercy upon them; give thanks for all He is going to do for them" (1 Tim. 2:1, TLB).

JESUS PRAYED FOR OTHERS

If we feel we minister in other ways, we may not feel the need to pray for people. Jesus—the Teacher, the Healer, the Counselor, the Friend, the Minister—prayed for others.

"My prayer is not for them alone. I pray also for those who will believe in me through their message" (John 17:20).

LET GOD TELL YOU WHO NEEDS PRAYER

God knows who needs your prayers, and He'll share that with you ... if you let Him.

During your devotional time:

Don't limit your prayer for others to whatever prayer list you may use. In your devotions, ask God to bring to mind anyone who needs prayer ... and then listen. Whoever comes to your mind, trust it is God's direction, and pray for them: family, acquaintances, strangers. The more control you give God here, the more He'll trust you with His people's needs.

In such a time of listening, God brought Sue to my mind. We had known each other casually in college, but that was eight years earlier. The rest of the week God continued to direct me to pray for Sue, with very specific instructions about something He wanted her to do. On Friday I felt God wanted me to tell her what He had shown me, even though she lived in California and I was in Oklahoma.

During the prayer time in my church's Sunday morning service, God again had me pray for Sue. At the end of the service, I looked down the aisle and was shocked. There was Sue!

An open and committed Christian, Sue met with me on Monday and invited me to share God's direction. I told her the problem God revealed to me and how He wanted her to pray about it. Sue smiled as she explained just how detailed God had been in His direction, and she shared the crucial need it applied to.

She felt the message was from God, and followed God's directives. She not only received His peace, but also through that peace Sue experienced miracles in other areas of her life.

During your day:

Ask God to show you people's needs and to help you respond with prayer:

. . .the sales clerk who is rude.

. . .the colleague who is tired.

. . .the family member who is struggling.

. . .the lonely looking stranger you pass on the sidewalk.

. . .the delivery man who is rushed.

. . .the child in the newspaper article.

It isn't necessary to know the background, the need, or even the person. God knows all that. It is necessary for us to notice the people around us and respond with prayer.

After the first session of a Prayerlife seminar, Carolyn left determined to try this idea of praying for strangers. She stopped by the grocery store before going home, and in the aisle was a woman with a crying infant. Before the seminar the next night, Carolyn excitedly told me, "Usually I'd just wish the baby would stop crying. But last night I prayed for him and his mother." Carolyn's face beamed. "By the time they got to the end of the aisle, the baby was laughing. Do you believe it! I've never even thought of doing anything like that before!"

Carolyn's love gift reached beyond the moment of prayer. She made an eternal investment in that mother and child.

> "As for me, far be it from me that I should sin against the
> Lord by failing to pray for you . . ." (1 Sam. 12:23a).

LET GOD TELL YOU WHEN TO PRAY FOR SOMEONE

Ask God to bring your loved ones and others to your mind whenever they need prayer. Then, when you think of them— whatever the context—pray for them. The more you respond to those thoughts with prayer, the more God will entrust you with others' needs.

In the midst of a personal and confidential struggle, there was a knock on the door. I opened it to see my brother and his family. After hugs and greetings, Ron asked me to go outside with him.

"Sis, I felt God wanted me to come pray with you, so here I am." Without knowing the problem, God gave Ron very specific directions. He prayed with me, stayed only a little while, then he and his family left. The drive was eight hours each way, so they'd drive all night to get back home.

I've never been free to tell Ron the details of my struggle, and he's never asked. But God knew when I needed prayer and told Ron, and Ron responded in obedience.

> "I have never stopped thanking God for you. I pray for you constantly, asking God, the glorious Father of our Lord Jesus Christ, to give you wisdom to see clearly and really understand who Christ is and all that He has done for you" (Eph. 1:16–17, TLB).

LET GOD TELL YOU WHAT TO PRAY FOR OTHERS

We often know the needs of those we pray for. Yet, even within those needs God will give us specific direction if we ask Him. But we tend to dictate to God—especially if the problem is serious or if we have prayed about it for a long time.

We usually pray in big blocks of requests. God usually guides us to pray for small specific steps.

After praying for several years for a certain person to become a Christian, God patiently taught me to put my requests in His hands and ask for His direction. He guided from step to step, and the results were astounding to me.

At a point in her life when she didn't even acknowledge the existence of God, God directed me to pray that someone with whom she had daily contact would become a Christian. After several months of praying, I received a phone call from my non-Christian friend. "Hi, Glaphré. Listen, the strangest thing happened—a man at work just became a Christian. Can you believe it? Anyway, he was telling me today he doesn't know what he's suppose to do now. So I told him I'd call you to find out."

She never knew I was crying as I answered her questions. That night I thanked God and asked Him, "What's next?"

> "So ever since we first heard about you we have kept on praying and asking God to help you understand what He

wants you to do, and to make you wise about spiritual things'' (Col. 1:9, TLB).

INHIBITORS OF THE LOVE GIFT OF PRAYER

1. Not really praying. Sometimes we say, "I'm praying for you" when we aren't. Sometimes we promise, "I'll sure pray for you" when we don't. We throw those phrases around glibly. It's become as common as saying, "Hi, how are you doing?"

Praying for someone is a great privilege and an awesome responsibility. If we say it, we need to *do* it. Listen to yourself. Be careful of your words.

2. Sharing confidential things. Much gossip happens in the name of prayer and prayer requests. Our unsaved loved ones know it. It's one more blockade God has to work through to help the very ones we are praying for. But this is a blockade *we* have built.

3. Negative praying. Allowing God to direct what we pray eliminates our tendency to pray negatively. It's easy to get lost in the burdens of our hearts, our concerns, and our fears for someone. To dwell on the negatives in the person or the situation instead of the potential is unfruitful.

A prayer of faith is a positive prayer—the opposite of negative praying. Present the negatives to God and allow Him to minister to your concerns. Then ask Him how to pray for the person, and pray a positive prayer of faith.

4. Our actions. Sometimes our sincere attempts to help those we pray for can interfere with the very things we long to happen. We have to stop playing God in each other's lives, instead we must ask God what He wants us to do.

. . . God may tell us to do nothing but pray. In the midst of real anxiety that can be the hardest direction, but God can help us to be obedient.

. . . God may tell us to do something that appears to have no redemptive value, such as offer to give a friend a night out and babysit her kids. Or give her daisies. But we can trust God's guidance.

. . . God may show us something in *us* that needs to be different. Listen to His revelations without being defensive. Obeying God's call to quit nagging, to be more positive—or whatever the direction—will be crucial if God is to continue His work through our prayers.

Praying for others is a love gift.

An eternal investment in their lives.

"God knows how often I pray for you. Day and night I bring you and your needs in prayer to the one I serve with all my might . . ." (Rom. 1:9, TLB).

PERSONAL DISCOVERIES IN PRAYER

1. Thank God for the privilege of praying for others.

2. Ask God to help you believe He will direct your prayers when you pray for others.

3. Ask God to help you sense others' needs and know how to pray for them.

4. Read Psalm 20:1.

5. Ask God to bring someone to your mind who is in distress, and pray for him or her.

6. Ask God to bring someone to your mind who needs protection, and pray for him or her.

7. Read Psalm 20:5.

8. Think of someone God has helped, and thank God for that help.

9. Read Psalm 20:6.

10. Thank God for the truth of that verse. Ask God to increase your faith in praying for others.

11. Ask God to bring to your mind a family member or close friend who especially needs help. Let God direct how you pray.

12. Ask God if anything in your life needs to change for your prayer for a specific person to be more effective. Let God guide your prayer.

13. Ask God if He wants you to do any special act of kindness for someone you've just prayed for. If God directs, complete that act of kindness this week.

14. Thank God for the loving people who are important to you.

SHARED DISCOVERIES IN PRAYER

A. As an entire group:

1. Read Philippians 1:19 in unison.

   "For I know that through your prayers and the help given by the Spirit of Jesus Christ, what has happened to me will turn out for my deliverance."

2. Share

   a. Have those who wish, share a time when someone's prayers made a real difference in their lives.

   b. Have those who wish, share how God expanded their prayers for others this week.

B. In groups of five people:

1. Read Colossians 1:3—4.

2. Those who wish, pray aloud for a new Christian.

3. Read Colossians 1:5—6.

4. Let God direct you in praying aloud for the ministry of your church.

5. Read Colossians 1:7–8.

6. Let God direct you in praying aloud for your pastor and any other ministers God brings to your mind. Feel free to pray several times.

7. Read Colossians 1:10.

8. Share with each other any help you need in being what you want to be in your home or at work. Pray aloud for each other. (Several could pray for each need.)

9. Read Colossians 1:11.

10. Share a family need. Pray aloud for each other's needs. (Several could pray for each need.)

11. Read Colossians 1:12–13.

12. Share concerns for any unsaved loved ones. Pray aloud for each other's loved ones. (Several could pray for each one.)

13. Share any special need you have in ministering to and loving your unsaved loved one. Pray aloud for each other.

C. As an entire group:

1. Read 1 Timothy 2:1.

2. Share personal needs with the group, and as many as feel led, pray aloud for that need.

   Note: The extra power from corporate prayer is not that one person prays and everyone else listens; it's that everyone is a part of that prayer in her heart and thoughts. *Pray in your hearts with whomever is leading in prayer.*

3. One person close in prayer: Thank God for the help He will be giving concerning all the needs shared.

4. Continue to pray for each other's needs this week.

9

HONEST PRAISE

Tear-stained whispers.
Loud cries of joy.
Heart-pulsed music.
Fasting with gladness.
A newly-carpeted Sunday-school room.
Telling a friend of God's kindness.
Heads bowed in silent worship.
Awed thoughts of God.
Feasting in the Psalms.
ALL EXPRESSIONS OF PRAISE.

God's admonition to praise Him requires our attention. This is no casual request. We're informed the rocks will open up and cry out praise to God if we don't. But observing the content of Christians' conversations and the tone of our spirits, there must be a lot of noisy rocks out there! (Luke 19:40.)

Praising God doesn't just happen. We don't wake up one morning and start praising Him automatically. We develop that awareness . . . that attitude . . . that heart-response. We learn to free our thoughts to soar to God in admiration, our words rising in acclamation.

Sometimes we're like young children tearing through our birthday gifts, barely noticing or appreciating the last gift we open before we rush on to see what's next. Sometimes our burden compels us to scurry on to think through our problem again . . . leaving God with a quick wave of "Thanks, but I can handle it." Or we wait to thank God until later—but then forget.

God knew about our forgetfulness, for reminders to praise Him weave through His Word.

GOD DESERVES OUR PRAISE

He is the Holy One. He is the One Whose love has opened a way to intimate fellowship with Him. This all-wise God, Who has a purpose for our lives, Who cares about all that touches us, Who created us, deserves our praise.

> "Give thanks unto the Lord, for He is good; His love endures for ever" (1 Chron. 16:34).

WE NEED TO PRAISE GOD

Praising God helps us remember the kind of God we have.
Praising God clears our focus.
Praising God reminds us of God's power.
Praising God restores perspective.
Praising God acknowledges to others God's sovereignty.
Praising God honors Him.
Praising God lifts us out of discouragement.

Praising God brings healing.
Praising God is something we were created for.
Praising God helps fulfill our purposes.

> "It is good to praise the Lord, and to make music to Your name, O Most High" (Ps. 92:1).

As a toddler develops his leg muscles, we have to develop our praise muscles.

PREPARING TO EXERCISE OUR PRAISE MUSCLES

Praise is not a game, neither is it a pretense. It isn't an attempt to fool God or ourselves with a programmed positive response. How could such a response be appreciated by God or fulfilling to us?

We prepare to exercise our praise muscles by being honest with God. "God, I really am grateful, I just forget to say it. Please teach me." Or, "God, I'm grateful in my head—but I don't *feel* it in my heart. Please help me." Or, "God, I'm not very grateful right now. I'm sorry. Please forgive me and help me."

THE BEGINNING EXERCISE FOR PRAISE MUSCLES

The first exercise is to learn to say "Thank You" to God.
. . . When you receive an act of kindness,
     say "Thank You" to God.
. . . When you feel the warmth and love of a friend or family member,
     say "Thank You" to God.
. . . When something works out great,
     say "Thank You" to God.
. . . When you look at a flower,
     say "Thank You" to God.
. . . When warm memories drift into your mind,
     say "Thank You" to God.

. . . When you think of the difference God makes in your life, say "Thank You" to God.

Saying "Thank You" to God throughout our day—even as we continue with our schedules—takes our focus off ourselves and our problems, and puts our attention onto God. It exercises our praise muscles.

AN ACTIVITY FOR OUR PRAISE MUSCLES

To help develop your praise muscles, select a daily activity; something you usually do without thinking. Let that activity remind you to praise God.

. . . Everytime you're at a red light, praise God.

. . . Everytime you brush your teeth, praise God.

. . . Everytime you dial the phone, praise God.

. . . Everytime you open a door, praise God.

. . . Everytime you see a smile, praise God.

Praising God needs to become a lifestyle. Not relegated to the end of your devotions, but an ongoing part of each day. An activity reminding you to praise God will help you begin that process. It develops your praise muscles.

PRAISE MUSCLES CAN CRAMP

When, in the midst of our own private trauma, we can find no reason to thank God . . . we do not have to force a false emotion on ourselves. Jesus didn't praise God that Lazarus was dead. He wept. Jesus didn't thank God for the cross. He struggled.

God doesn't yank you into praising Him when you have a muscle cramp. He wants to minister to that cramp. Our tendency is to nurse our hurt muscle, often forgetting that— even in the midst of trauma—we can be thankful we have the kind of God we do.

If we don't even feel that, we can pray:

"God, I'm so absorbed in this hurt, I'm having trouble appreciating *You*. Please help me."

A PRAISE PROJECT

As leg muscles become stronger, a child attempts running and skating; an adult jogger may move on to running marathons. A praise project stretches our muscles as we purposefully bring attention to God through our gratitude.

When you're especially aware of God's goodness, or when He's helped in an unusual way, plan a praise project, a praise gift. It might be something as simple as telling a friend about your wonderful God. It might be a special way to show God and others your gratitude to Him. As your praise muscles develop, plan special praise projects for God.

. . . One family recarpeted a Sunday school room when a run-away child returned home. It was a praise project.

. . . One man gives a gift to God each year on the anniversary of the day God healed him of a terminal illness. It's a gift of praise.

Fasting is an active part of our family's life; we participate in each other's concerns and burdens through fasting. But we also participate in praising God together through fasting.

When God answered a prayer our family had prayed for ten years, each of us did our own version of fasting. For one week my fourteen-year-old sister gave up her daily taco feeds after school with her friends. This was part of our family desire to show God the depth of our gratitude.

> "You are my God, and I will give you thanks; you are my God, and I will exalt You" (Ps. 118:28).

Exercised praise muscles make every part of our lives stronger; strong enough to freely include God in our thoughts, our conversations, our attitudes, our activities. Praising God—as a lifestyle—honors Him.

PERSONAL DISCOVERIES IN PRAYER

1. Read Psalm 96:1–6.

   Ask God to guide you in completing the following:

   a. The most difficult time of the day for me to have a spirit of praise: _____

   b. The easiest time of the day for me to have a spirit of praise: _____

   c. My main obstacles to praise: _____

   _____

2. Read Psalm 96:7–9.

   a. Ask God to show you any place in your life you currently have a praise "muscle cramp."

   b. Let God minister to you and help you thank Him that He is still *your* God.

3. Read Psalm 96:10–12.

   a. With God's guidance, select an activity to serve as a reminder to praise God: _____

   _____

   b. Ask God to help you remember to praise Him.

4. Read Psalm 21:1.

   Praise God for His attributes. Be specific.

5. Read Psalm 21:2.

   Thank God for previous answers to prayers. (They don't need to be recent.)

6. Read Psalm 21:5–6.

a. Praise God for the blessings He has given others. Be specific.

b. Praise God for the blessings He has given you. Be specific.

c. Tell God about the joy you have because you belong to Him.

7. Read Psalm 21:7.

   Write out this verse putting your name in place of "the king."

   _____

   _____

   _____

   _____

8. Read Hebrews 13:15–16. Plan a special praise project. Perhaps you could write a friend, telling her of God's kindness to you. Work out the details with God; make specific plans to complete this as soon as possible.

SHARED DISCOVERIES IN PRAYER

A. As an entire group:

1. Read Psalm 33:1–5.

2. Make a list of some favorite songs of praise.

3. Select one of the songs and sing it together as a prayer of praise.

4. Have various women share what God taught them this past week about praising Him.

B. In groups of eight to ten people:

1. Have each woman share the easiest and the most difficult time for her to praise God. What makes the difference?

2. Give individuals a chance to share what activities they selected to remind them to praise God. Did they help?

3. Memorize

   a. Read this Scripture aloud in unison:

   "Say thank you to the Lord for being so good, for always being so loving and kind" (Ps. 107:1, TLB).

   b. Going around your circle, have each person say one word of the verse until the verse has been completed and each person has said one word.

   c. Repeat "b" three times, with each saying her word from memory. Begin with a different person each time.

   d. Say the verse in unison from memory.

   e. Each who will, try to say the verse alone from memory.

   f. Say it again in unison.

4. Read Psalm 111:1.

5. As many as wish to, tell God aloud how you feel about Him; praise Him for being the kind of God He is.

6. Read Psalm 111:2.

7. As many as wish to, thank God aloud for a specific part of His creation and tell Him why you like it.

8. Read Psalm 111:3.

9. Each person thank God aloud for some recent help He has given you.

10. Read Psalm 111:4.

11. Each woman thank God aloud for special help He has recently given a loved one.

12. Read Psalm 111:5.

13. Each individual thank God aloud for a time when He provided something you needed.

C. As an entire group:

1. Sing another song of praise.

2. Discuss

    a. Why should we praise God?

    _____

    b. What difference does praising God make in *us?*

    _____

    _____

3. Read Psalm 103:1−2.

4. Look over the items listed below. All who feel led, praise God by sharing with the group God's help in the following: (As time allows, feel free to share several times.)

    a. Comfort

    b. Special guidance

    c. Healing

    d. Help with your children

    e. Help in your marriage

    f. Special material provision

    g. Protection

    h. A loved one accepting Christ

    i. A discovery you've made about God

    j. Anything else God brings to your mind

5. Review your memory verse.

6. Close by singing another song of praise.

10

WHEN GOD DOESN'T ANSWER

When we feel God's help has been distant for so long,
   the resulting clouds of despair seem to even interfere
      with God's Presence . . .
When we've done all we know to do,
   but we can't see that it has done any good . . .
When God doesn't answer . . .
      We need to ask Him, "Why?"
God will reveal *our* part in getting rid of the clouds, the
barriers, the obstructions in our fellowship with Him.

DISOBEYING

The most common hindrance to prayer is disobedience.
Often we know what the disobedience is, so we purposely
avoid looking at this potential barrier. But God will not
partake in our games or excuses. Our disobedience blocks
both our prayers and God's freedom to help us.

Disobedience could be doing something we shouldn't, or *not* doing something we should. We cannot measure disobedience by comparing our lives with others', but according to God's personal revelation to our own hearts. We are required to live in the light God has shown *us*.

Here we cannot rely on our memories or our conscience. We must give the Holy Spirit permission to search our hearts and show us anything that—for whatever reason—we are not seeing.

> "Search me, O God, and know my heart; test my thoughts. Point out anything you find in me that makes you sad . . ." (Ps. 139:23–24, TLB).

If we confess the disobedience, ask for and accept God's forgiveness, and ask God's help to obey, His power is once again free to work.

> "Jesus replied, 'Because I will only reveal myself to those who love me and *obey* me . . .' " (John 14:23, TLB).

TRUSTING IN SOMETHING OR SOMEONE BESIDES GOD

Even when we begin a concentrated effort to focus on God, slippage can take place. Sometimes without realizing it
. . . we look to others for the answers.
. . . we begin dictating to God instead of listening for His guidance.
. . . we trust the existing circumstances more than God's power.

God will show us where our focus is, what we are trusting in. God will help us believe more in Him and in His power than in anything or anyone else.

"I lift up my eyes to the hills; where does my help come from? My help comes from the Lord . . ." (Ps. 121:1–2a).

UNWILLING TO ACCEPT THE DISCIPLINE OF CONTINUALLY PRAYING.

The Bible gives us examples of people praying persistently until they get all the help they need. Jesus Himself tells us to do just that in two rather lengthy examples (Luke 11:5–8; 18:1–8).

When you are discouraged, you need to pause, tell God you're discouraged, and let Him minister to you. God will comfort you. Lift your load. Encourage you. Then equip you to continue praying.

If you're no longer sure your request is what God wants—then stop. Check it through with God again. And pray accordingly.

If you're spiritually lazy and get bored or impatient with carrying a burden of prayer for any length of time, then ask God's help. He'll increase your concern, your belief in God's power, and your willingness to let Him help you establish a stronger discipline.

"Don't be weary in prayer; keep at it . . . " (Col. 4:2, TLB).

HARBORING A NEGATIVE OR CRITICAL SPIRIT

At first glance these two may seem like the same thing; they're not. But each invades our prayers and makes them less effective.

A negative person lives in an atmosphere of gloom. Whenever something joyful or positive happens, a negative person immediately sees it through her cloudy version of cheerless reality. Hers is a moody state of mind. She has a despondent condition of the heart—a saddened approach to life. Somehow life's bumps and turns have chased the light away . . . leaving only shadows.

A critical person feels a need to cut everything and everyone down to a manageable size. She uses a piercing ray gun of fault-finding, ever on the search to expose flaws. She's a self-appointed judge who censors and blames and scorns— often behind the cloak of spirituality.

It's possible for us to get so used to our negative nature or critical spirit that we no longer see those things in ourselves. If we would allow Him, God would reveal our nature to us. . . . God will enter the shadows of negativity. His light will fill the dark places. Heal the despair. Begin creating joy.

. . . God will relieve critical people of the quest to expose. He'll put His love for others in our hearts and free us to trust others to Him. He'll help us forgive our own imperfections.

> "Fix your thoughts on what is true and good and right. Think about things that are pure and lovely, and dwell on the fine, good things in others. Think about all you can praise God for and be glad about" (Phil. 4:8, TLB).
>
> "Blessed are the merciful, for they will be shown mercy" (Matt. 5:7).

INTERFERING BY SATAN

We have nothing to fear from Satan. God is more powerful, and *we are God's!* But one of Satan's tricks is to make himself invisible. Not seeing him, we forget he is a present force committed to interfering with God's purposes.

We need to ask, in Jesus' name, for protection from Satan's interferences.

> "Jesus said to him, 'Away from me, Satan! For it is written: "Worship the Lord your God, and serve him only" ' " (Matt. 4:10).

"The Lord said to Satan, 'The Lord rebuke you, Satan!
The Lord, who has chosen Jerusalem, rebuke you! . . .' "
(Zech. 3:2).

"My prayer is not that you take them out of the world but
that you protect them from the evil one" (John 17:15).

SUFFERING FROM EMOTIONAL EXHAUSTION

Carrying a burden for a long time can wear you out. When
the emptiness of a new loss won't quit hurting . . . when
babies are sick and have been crying for days . . . when work
is especially stressful . . . when schedules have run out of
control . . .

After the physical exhaustion comes something which
affects us even more: *emotional exhaustion.*

When that's where you are . . .

You need to stop and let God minister to you.

Don't pray for others just now. Let God minister to you.

Don't pray for the problem just now. Let God minister to
you.

"Come to me and I will give you rest—all of you who
work so hard beneath a heavy yoke" (Matt. 11:28, TLB).

Ask God to refresh you,
   then take a nap
      as God ministers to you.
Put up your feet,
   ask God to restore you,
      close your eyes, and be still in God's Presence.
Take a walk or look out a window,
   ask God to heal the damaging effects of the circumstances,
      and look at God's creation.

"He will be gentle—He will not shout nor quarrel in the streets. He will not break the bruised reed, nor quench the dimly burning flame. He will encourage the faint-hearted, those tempted to despair" (Isa. 42:2–3a, TLB).

WHEN WHAT WE MOST DREAD HAPPENS ... EVEN THOUGH WE PRAYED

What happens when we did all we knew to do, listened and heard and obeyed—yet, the very thing we persistently pleaded against happens anyway? We search and search . . . but there is absolutely no explanation that makes any sense.

Then, as always, we tell God how we feel:

"God, I'm crushed. Why did you let me down? I feel like you betrayed me."

"My God, my God, why have you forsaken me? Why do you refuse to help me or even listen to my groans?" (Ps. 22:1–2, TLB).

"God, please . . . please do something about the hurt . . . the darkness."

"So do not fear for I am with you; do not be dismayed, for I am your God . . ." (Isa. 41:10).

"God, help me give You my need to know the answer, to understand."

"Even when walking through the dark valley of death I will not be afraid, for you are close beside me, guarding, guiding all the way" (Ps. 23:4, TLB).

"God, please help me believe in *You* more than in what has happened!"

". . . I know whom I have believed, and am convinced that He is able to guard what I have entrusted to Him for that day" (2 Tim. 1:12).

PERSONAL DISCOVERIES IN PRAYER

(This devotional may be completed in one day or over several days.)

1. Read Psalm 91:1–6, 14–16.

   a. Ask God to help you feel so secure in His Presence that you can give Him the freedom to reveal whatever He wishes to you.

   b. Give God permission to reveal any hindrances to prayer in your life as you complete this devotional. (Spend as much time here as you need before going on.)

2. Read Psalm 32:1–5.

   a. Ask God to show you any spiritual failure in your life. Ask for and receive God's forgiveness.

   b. Thank God for His revelations and His forgiveness.

3. Read Deuteronomy 5:13; 13:4.

   a. Ask God to show you any disobedience in your life. Talk with Him about it.

4. Read Matthew 6:14–15.

   a. Ask God to show you anyone you need to forgive. Listen without offering justification or excuse. Allow God to help you forgive.

   b. If you did forgive, thank God for helping you to forgive.

   c. If no one specific comes to mind, ask God to help you always have a forgiving spirit.

   d. If someone did come to your mind, but you can't yet honestly forgive, ask God to help you *want* to forgive.

5. Read 1 Corinthians 13:4–7; 1 Peter 2:1.

   a. Ask God to show you any critical or negative tendencies within you. Allow God to be specific.

   b. If the criticism is directed toward specific people, ask God to help you see those people the way He does. Ask Him to fill you with His love for them.

   c. Think of the light of God entering your thoughts and heart and chasing away the shadows of past criticism and negativity.

   d. Ask God to heal the effects of your past problems in this area. Ask God to heal those you have hurt and to heal your own spirit.

   e. Ask God to teach you how to break these negative and critical habits.

   f. Thank God for His desire that you be free of these problems.

   g. Thank God for His help.

6. Read Isaiah 61:1–4.

   a. Present to God any area of your life in which you are emotionally weary.

   b. Read this Scripture again, as if God's healing, restoring words are directed to you personally.

   c. Relax, close your eyes, and allow God to begin to restore you.

   d. Sometime in the next two days take a slow walk, or sit looking out a window. Don't talk over your problem again—just ask God to minister to you. Be quiet inside and let Him restore you.

e. At some later time, ask God one thing you could change to help you not become so weary.

SHARED DISCOVERIES IN PRAYER

A. As an entire group:

1. Have everyone look up and one person read Psalm 13.

2. Discuss

   a. What are the potential dangers when your prayers seem to be unanswered? _____

   _____

   _____

   b. What could we do to avoid these dangers? _____

   _____

   _____

3. Read Luke 11:5–8; 18:1–8.

4. Discuss

   a. Why do we quit praying for something? _____

   _____

   b. What do these Scriptures say about those reasons?

   _____

   _____

   c. When would it be right to quit praying for something?

   _____

5. Read Colossians 4:2.

6. According to Matthew 6:12, what is one criteria for our sins being forgiven?

_____

_____

7. Discuss

   a. What are some of the reasons we use for not forgiving
      someone? _____

   _____

   b. What do Matthew 6:14–15 and Matthew 18:21–22
      say about our reasons for not forgiving others? _____

   _____

   c. What does 1 John 2:9–11 say about not forgiving?
      How does this affect our prayers? _____

   _____

8. Have a time of silent prayer. Each listen to God. Is there
   someone you need to forgive? Let God help you forgive
   that person now—at least ask God to help you *want* to
   forgive this person.

9. Read Psalm 61:1–4.

10. Discuss

    a. What kind of conditions can wear us out emotional-
       ly? _____

    _____

    b. How can this affect our prayers? _____

    _____

11. Read Isaiah 50:10.

B. In groups of three to five people:

1. Share a problem you are having with a specific prayer request, e.g., having trouble praying consistently, tired of praying for it, etc. Pray for each other.

2. Share a personal problem there seems to be no answer for. Several pray for each other's problems.

C. As an entire group:

1. Share experiences when it seemed God wasn't answering prayers, yet His answer did come. Also, share times when God's answers were different from the ones you wanted—and remarkably better.

2. How might we respond if, after we've prayed, the thing we most feared happens anyway?

3. In those times of darkness, without the answer we long for, we need God's help to trust Him.

   a. Read Isaiah 41:10.

   b. Share experiences when God was faithful in times of loss and darkness.

   c. Read Psalm 63:6–8.

4. Ask a person who has walked with God through one of those dark times to lead the group in a closing prayer.

11

WHAT DO YOU WANT WHEN YOU PRAY?

When did it happen? When did we become hedonistic Christians? When did we become consumed with making our lives easy and pleasurable?

We eagerly grab the special formulas that promise quick and effortless success. We clutch to stories of Christians who have "made it" and live the easy life. We wave these stories and formulas at each other to pump up our faith so we also can "have it all." We spread the promises of carefree living before God and wait for Him to get busy and deliver our dreams. Dreams we want. Dreams we're convinced will make us happy. When God has done "this" for us . . . then . . . then our lives will be what we need and long for them to be.

Rarely does God break into our self-seeking prayers with His revelations for us. He'll not force them on us. Through His Word He tells us our mission, His vision for us. Now . . .

He waits for us to be interested . . . to care . . . to ask for a personal application . . . to accept our assignment and get to work.

Rarely does God show us detailed blueprints for our part in His mission. Upon request, He'll reveal a step or two, steps we must follow before we can see the next few steps.

> "For I have come down from heaven not to do my will but to do the will of him who sent me" (John 6:38).

THE DIRECTION

> "But seek first his kingdom and his righteousness, and all these things will be given to you as well" (Matt. 6:33).

Seek God *first*. Its simplicity seems to negate its importance. Its complexity is beyond human understanding.

We may have to ask God to help us *want* to seek Him first. We may need to ask God to teach us *how*. But His directive is clear. Understanding what His directive means to us personally and following it is a function of prayer. It's also preparation for receiving God's specific mission for us.

THE COMMAND

> "My command is this: Love each other as I have loved you" (John 15:12).

We must love beyond ourselves. Beyond our family. Beyond our friends. Beyond our church. Beyond . . . to give our love gift of prayer to others.

Have you let God give you a burden of love for anyone outside your circle? Is there a country, a family, a child, a need . . . beyond . . . that you pray about? Or, is your praying only for your own comfort? Your own family? Your own church?

THE EXPLANATION

"Greater love has no one than this, that one lay down his life for his friends. You are my friends if you do what I command. . . . You did not choose me, but I chose you to go and bear fruit—fruit that will last. Then the Father will give you whatever you ask in my name. This is my command: Love each other" (John 15:13–14, 16–17).

You . . . you. Not your minister. Not your husband. Not a respected church leader. *You* are chosen.

To be fulfilled—yes.
But more than that!
Beyond that . . .
You are chosen to bear fruit.

Beyond your personal needs . . . do you pray for God to equip you to "bear fruit that will last"?

THE CALL

"But you will receive power when the Holy Spirit comes on you; and you will be my witnesses in Jerusalem, and in all Judea and Samaria, and to the ends of the earth" (Acts 1:8).

Is this commission too abstract to get hold of? Too general to know what to do with? Too big to apply to us?

So what do we do? Dismiss it? Isn't the Call too important not to discover its personal application?

We can orchestrate grand schemes of how God's purposes should be fulfilled in our lives. The plan may receive great applause for its merit. But whose plan is it?

By my bed is a mug with pencils and pens in it. It's special because my niece Christa gave it to me. It works great as a pencil holder, but that is *not* what it was created for.

It doesn't matter that much if a mug isn't used for its intended purpose. But what about us? Dare *we* decide how to personalize God's call? Or should we ask our Creator His intended purpose for our lives?

The details are revealed as we seek God. Not just initially, but continually. It's possible to receive beginning instructions and then assume how to develop them—and act on *our* assumptions.

Beyond our plans . . . are God's.

> " 'For my thoughts are not your thoughts, neither are your ways my ways,' declares the Lord'' (Isa. 55:8).

THE BEGINNING

We begin where we are. We present our responsibilities, our interests, our opportunities, our strengths to God. As we ask God to fulfill His mission for us, He will.

. . . Ruthie was shy when it came to telling others about her God. She presented her kitchen redecorating project to God. He gave ideas how to make one wall arrangement an opportunity to talk about Him. Ruthie excitedly followed the ideas. Now guests, delivery men, whoever enters her kitchen, asks about her pictures. Her explanation tells how her God has changed her life. A beginning.

. . . In her devotions, as Lin read Scriptures about the fruit of God's Word, she felt a burden for those who live in countries that don't allow Bibles. "I feel when I read my Bible, I'm to ask God to reveal the truth of what I'm reading to those unable to get Bibles." It's a beginning.

. . . Secretaries: You could pray for everyone to whom you address an envelope. It's a beginning.

. . . Housekeepers: You could pray for people who live or work in the places you clean. It's a beginning.

. . . Teachers: You could pray regularly for each child. It's a beginning.

. . . Gardeners: You could ask God to use His creation to reveal Himself to others. It's a beginning.

. . . Painters: You could pray over your pictures and ask God to use them to draw people to Him. It's a beginning.

. . . Real estate agents: You could pray in each home you show, asking God to help people sense Him there with you. It's a beginning.

Whatever your responsibilities or projects or work . . . seek God's purpose for it. From that beginning, God will reveal the next step.

THE PRIVILEGE

> "I have brought you glory on earth by completing the work you gave me to do" (John 17:4).

We are offered the privilege of honoring God. The honor intended for God through our lives is not possible unless we put aside our continued attention to our own desires. It's not possible unless we change direction away from ourselves and toward God, obey the command, accept the call, seek God's vision for *us*, and embrace the privilege of honoring God.

> ". . . I consider everything a loss compared to the surpassing greatness of knowing Christ Jesus my Lord . . ." (Phil. 3:8).

PERSONAL DISCOVERIES IN PRAYER

1. Read Matthew 6:33.

   a. Ask God to show you what or who you seek instead of God. List what God reveals to you.

   _____

   _____

b. Tell God your feelings about seeking Him *first*.

c. Ask God to show you one thing or one priority that has to change if you are to seek Him first.

_____

d. Make a commitment to God concerning what He has just shown you.

e. Ask God, in Jesus' name, to teach you to seek Him first.

2. Read John 15:12.

a. Ask God to show you anything that hinders you from following this command. Ask Him to help you.

b. Allow God to help you see how much of your praying and activities are for self-comfort. Write what you see here.

_____

_____

_____

c. Ask God to give you His burden of love, or to help you be willing to receive His burden of love.

d. Ask God to bring to your mind a need you've never prayed for before. (Example: world hunger, missing children, physically abused women, unemployed, etc.) Pray for that need as God directs.

e. Thank God for sharing His love for others through *you*.

3. Read Acts 1:8; Isaiah 55:8–9.

a. Pray, as God directs, for a neighbor you have never prayed for before.

b. Ask God's direction as you look through a newspaper or magazine and pray for people or problems reported there.

c. Pray for someone who has taught you about spiritual matters.

d. Ask God to bring a foreign country to your mind, and pray as He directs.

e. Give to God all of your personal responsibilities and seek His purposes for those responsibilities. Write here any specific ideas He gives you.

_____

_____

_____

_____

f. Thank God for wanting you to seek Him.

SHARED DISCOVERIES IN PRAYER

A. As an entire group:

1. Read Matthew 6:33 in unison:

   "But seek first his kingdom and his righteousness, and all these things will be given to you as well."

2. Everyone pray silently, asking God to release His power in *you* in this session.

3. What does Jesus say His purpose is in John 6:38?

   _____

   _____

4. What is Jesus' specific mission relating to that purpose? John 6:40.

_____

_____

5. What part would Jesus' attitude in John 5:30 and 12:49−50 have in the fulfillment of questions 3 and 4?

_____

_____

_____

6. Did Jesus ever struggle over His purpose and mission? How did He handle the struggle? John 12:26−28.

_____

_____

_____

7. What did Jesus tell God in John 17:4?

_____

_____

8. Discuss

a. How much do we believe that Jesus' purpose is *our* life's purpose? What other things do we tend to accept as our purpose instead?

b. How important is prayer in making Jesus' purpose for our lives *our* purpose?

B. In groups of eight people:

1. Read Philippians 2:5−11.

2. What is the relationship between verses 6−8 and 9−11?

_____

3. This Scripture says our attitude should be like Christ's.
   What does that mean?

   _____

   _____

4. Each person pray silently. Ask God for His special
   wisdom and discernment for the next sharing and
   discussion.

5. Share with each other a personal responsibility or
   project you would like God to be honored through.

   a. Have the group brainstorm briefly on ideas of how
      God could be honored in each person's responsibility
      or project mentioned.

   b. After all have shared, have everyone pray silently.
      Give God the ideas discussed for your project. Ask
      Him to show you how to honor Him in this
      responsibility.

6. All who wish to, pray aloud for each item listed below
   before the group goes on to the next item. Allow God to
   guide you as you pray.

   a. Pray for a stranger you've seen recently.

   b. Pray for a specific need for your church that you've
      never prayed for before.

   c. Pray for someone in government.

   d. Pray for a group of people who are hurting (e.g.,
      children who are mistreated, people out of work,
      people who are hungry, etc.).

C. As an entire group:

1. Share anything God has shown you in this study concerning glorifying Him instead of merely seeking your own comfort.

2. Have one person read Philippians 3:7–8 as a closing prayer.

12

FOLLOWING THE PATTERN

It's possible for something to become so familiar to us that we don't pay any attention to it. Often, the Lord's Prayer is that way. When we say it aloud in a group, that's what we usually do—*say* it, rather than *pray* it. We "say" it, trying to make sure we get all the words correct so that we don't embarrass ourselves in front of the people standing nearest us.

When we come across the Lord's Prayer in the Bible, it's easy to skim over it quickly. After all, we can even repeat it from memory . . . so we don't need to read it carefully.

But the Lord's Prayer contains a pattern for our individual prayer times. Perhaps one reason it seems antiquated is that *our* prayers don't usually follow its pattern. We tend to tell God "Hi" and rush frantically down the list of things we want Him to *do* for us. Telling God of personal needs is not the first, or even the second item in Jesus' prayers. Personal requests are the *fourth* item in Jesus' model prayer. We can rarely wait that long! To us, everything else seems superfluous compared with telling God our problems.

But then, we don't always have the attitude of the disciples. At that moment they weren't saying, "God, this is what we want You to do for us—please hurry!" They were requesting, "Lord, teach us to pray."

If we'd back up and ask the same question, God's response would be to lead us into a more effective fellowship with Him.

In this chapter I'd like us to use the Lord's Prayer as a pattern.

PERSONAL DISCOVERIES IN PRAYER

1. Ask God to teach you to pray.

2. Ask God to bring to your mind one problem you are now facing—a problem God wants you to present to Him during this brief study of the Lord's Prayer. (You'll be using the same problem throughout this chapter.) Don't decide on your own, but allow God to guide your decision. *(Take the time to receive that guidance from God before you continue.)*

"OUR FATHER WHICH ART IN HEAVEN . . ." (Matt. 6:9)

This beginning isn't a hello-wave to God from Jesus on His way to more important matters. This is the first step of prayer: realizing you are in God's Presence.

It's true that God is around us and always with us, but we're not always aware of His Presence . . . and we need to sense God's Presence if our prayer time is to be meaningful.

How long we take to realize God's Presence depends on how preoccupied we are with other things. If we are going to have a ten-minute prayer time and have to spend seven of those minutes on this first step, the remaining three minutes will be much more effective praying than if we had skipped this step.

1. Pray this first phrase of our Lord's pattern for prayer: "Our Father which art in heaven."

2. Think of your favorite outdoor scene. Get the picture clearly in your mind. Be specific.

3. Now realize that your God created this scene.

4. Think of the power and specific involvement it took from God to create this scene.

5. Think of yourself in that scene with the problem God has guided you to present during these prayer times.

6. Thank God for His Presence.

7. Pray again that beginning phrase: "Our Father which art in heaven."

"HALLOWED BE THY NAME" (Matt. 6:9)

Here, Jesus verbally recognizes that God is holy. This is the second step of prayer: worshiping God. Here we spend time thinking about the kind of God we have. His goodness. His majesty. His purity. His power. His holiness.

This part of the prayer pattern is to get better acquainted with God and to correct our misconceptions about Him. This is a time when God enlarges our understanding of Him; when He reminds us of the kind of God we belong to.

The better we know God,
    the easier it is to trust Him.
The more we trust Him,
    the easier it is to obey Him.

1. Pray this second phrase in our Lord's pattern for prayer: "Hallowed be Thy Name."

2. Read Psalm 36:5–9.

3. Think of some specific times when you've seen God's goodness in your life. List them here.

   _____

   _____

   _____

4. Thank God for sharing His goodness with you.

5. Think of some specific times when you've seen God's goodness in the lives of those you care about. List them here.

   _____

   _____

   _____

6. Thank God for sharing His goodness with those you love.

7. Think of one example of God's power. List it here.

   _____

8. Think that *this same God* is with you now and knows your problem. Think of this same power and goodness of God surrounding you and your problem.

9. Pray again the phrase: "Hallowed be Thy Name."

"THY KINGDOM COME, THY WILL BE DONE IN EARTH AS IT IS IN HEAVEN" (Matt. 6:10)

It's so easy to tell God what to do, to forget *He* is in charge, not *us*. The more distraught we are, the easier it is to dictate to God what He should do about our situation. The longer we've lived with a problem, the easier it is to give up and conclude that it's hopeless—not even God can do anything about this.

"Thy will be done" is not a sad prayer of resignation. It's a beautiful, wondrous reality—God cares enough to *have* a will concerning us.

1. Pray this third phrase to God: "Thy kingdom come, Thy will be done in earth as it is in heaven."

2. Ask God to help you believe He has a solution for the problem you are presenting to Him.

3. Ask God to help you trust His will concerning this problem.

4. Ask God to help you *want* His will concerning this problem.

5. Ask God to reveal to you at least one thing He wants you to pray for or do concerning this problem. Don't tell God what to do but seek *His* will. (This may take some time. Be willing to spend as much time here with God as necessary.) Make notes of God's direction.

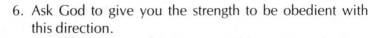

_____

_____

_____

6. Ask God to give you the strength to be obedient with this direction.

7. Thank God that He will resolve your problem.

8. Pray this phrase again: "Thy kingdom come, Thy will be done, in earth as it is in heaven."

"GIVE US THIS DAY OUR DAILY BREAD" (Matt. 6:11)

Once we have yielded ourselves to God's will . . . and we feel we can trust His care . . . then we can freely ask: "God, supply my needs."

Sometimes we feel embarrassed about a need, so we tuck it away instead of presenting it to God. Sometimes we feel a problem is so unsolvable there's no point in bringing it to God.

Nothing is too small, nothing too big to present to God. We just need to remember not to dictate to God what to do, but present our needs to Him and leave them in His powerful hands.

1. Pray this phrase of Jesus' pattern: "Give us this day our daily bread."

2. Tell God your needs, particularly concerning the specific problem you are presenting to Him. Ask for God's help.

3. Pray again the phrase: "Give us this day our daily bread."

"FORGIVE US OUR DEBTS, AS WE FORGIVE OUR DEBTORS" (Matt. 6:12)

There are two important rules we must follow if our prayers are to be effective: we must receive forgiveness; we must give forgiveness. Neglecting these rules is like building a dam that blocks the flow of the river. Lack of forgiveness blocks the flow of God's ability to work through our prayers.

"Forgive Us Our Debts . . . "

No excuses will work here. No comparisons to others, no speeding by these words. Instead we must deliberately give God permission to show us anything we need forgiveness for, then we must ask for and receive His forgiveness.

1. Pray this phrase of the Lord's Prayer: "Forgive us our debts."

2. Ask God to help you feel secure in His Presence, even with His knowledge of your sins and shortcomings.

3. As it relates to your problem, give God permission to specifically reveal to you anything for which you need to ask His forgiveness. Don't rush. Don't dismiss anything that comes to your mind. Don't give excuses or try to explain away anything.

4. Ask God's forgiveness for whatever He brings to your mind.

5. Thank God for His forgiveness.

". . . As We Forgive Our Debtors."

The prayer isn't: "As we forgive people after our problems with them are solved." Or, "As we forgive all people except those who are really unpleasant." It doesn't say we're to forgive people if they don't hurt us anymore . . . Jesus simply says that *as* we forgive, we are forgiven.

1. As it relates to your problem, give God permission to specifically reveal to you anyone you need to forgive. Again, don't rush. Don't make excuses. Just accept what God shows you.

2. With Jesus' help, forgive those God has brought to your mind.

3. Pray a prayer for healing in the relationships God has brought to your mind.

4. Thank God for His faithfulness to you in revealing these things.

5. Pray this phrase again: "Forgive us our debts, as we forgive our debtors."

"AND LEAD US NOT INTO TEMPTATION, BUT DELIVER US FROM EVIL ... " (Matt. 6:13)

Ideally, we don't wait until we are at the crossroads of temptation to pray this prayer. It's a prayer for protection that begins before we even approach temptation. "God, help me sense Your protection every moment." This is a prayer born out of Satan's continual attempts to thwart our desire to follow God, to muffle God's voice, and to interfere with our obedience to God.

The more we grow in our fellowship with our God, the more subtle and disguised Satan's plans for us become. Only by God, with God, and through God are we delivered. Because of God we need have no fear. Realizing our need for God's deliverance, we can appropriate God's protective power through prayer.

1. Pray this phrase of the Lord's patterned prayer: "And lead us not into temptation, but deliver us from evil."

2. Ask God to reassure you of *His* power in the face of evil.

3. Ask God to help you believe His power is available to *you*.

4. Ask God to reveal to you your temptations in your problem. Ask Him to help you see these temptations clearly. Spend time listening.

5. Ask God to show you what disciplines you need to establish in your thoughts, your conversations, your actions, or your attitudes—disciplines that will strengthen you in these specific areas of temptation. Listen for God's direction.

6. Make some specific plans with God concerning these areas of discipline. Make notes here.

_____

_____

7. Ask God to help you establish these disciplines.

8. Pray this phrase again: "And lead us not into temptation, but deliver us from evil."

"FOR THINE IS THE KINGDOM AND THE POWER AND THE GLORY FOREVER ... " (Matt. 6:13)

Jesus concludes His prayer much as He began it, and so should we: bringing full attention to God. At this point you can almost feel the swelling of worship and adoration as Jesus declares that glory belongs to God and God alone.

1. Pray the phrase: "For Thine is the kingdom and the power and the glory forever."

2. Express to God your trust in Him.

3. Express to God your desire that He be glorified in the world.

4. Express to God your desire that He be glorified in *your life*.

5. Express to God your desire that He be glorified in your problem.

6. Pray this phrase again: "For Thine is the kingdom and the power and the glory forever."

"AMEN"

"Amen" communicates: "So be it, Lord. It's Yours! I release my problem to Your care. I leave it there. I believe it! I believe *You*, God!" What a releasing way to leave a prayer time. God is in charge!

1. Think of Jesus in front of you with His hands open toward you.

2. Think of yourself putting your problem into Jesus' hands.

3. Think of taking your hands away and leaving the problem in His hands.

4. Pray this prayer: "So be it, Lord. It is Yours."

5. Repeat this last word: "Amen."

6. Pray the Lord's prayer in its entirety, *as a prayer* (Matt. 6:9–13).

7. Thank God for giving you a prayer pattern and for beginning to teach you how to follow it.

SHARED DISCOVERIES IN PRAYER

A. As an entire group:

1. Have everyone look up Psalm 71:15–16, assigning one person to read it aloud.

2. To help, encourage, teach, and inspire each other to continue developing your prayer lives, in this session you will share what God has taught you through the chapters of this study book.

   a. Read Psalm 25:4–5.

   b. Have one person lead in prayer—asking that this be a time of encouragement and help to each other and a time of glorifying God.

   CHAPTER 1 "CAN PRAYER REALLY HELP?"

   a. Read Psalm 34:17.

   b. Have several people share what God taught them while studying chapter 1. (Refer to your notes in Chapter 1 to refresh your memory.)

CHAPTER 2 "SECURE IN THE RELATIONSHIP"

a. Read Psalm 34:22.

b. Several share personal lessons God taught you in chapter 2.

CHAPTER 3 "THE RIGHT DIRECTION"

a. Read Psalm 34:15.

b. Review the memory verse, Psalm 46:10.

c. Share the lessons God taught in chapter 3.

B. In groups of three to four people:

Share any personal needs relating to these first three chapters and pray for each other concerning these needs.

C. As an entire group, review these chapters:

CHAPTER 4 "A UNIQUELY PERSONAL FRIENDSHIP"

a. Read Psalm 34:8–10.

b. Share lessons God taught you while you were covering chapter 4.

CHAPTER 5 "WHAT DO YOU HEAR?"

a. Read Psalm 34:11.

b. Share lessons God taught you while you were studying chapter 5.

CHAPTER 6 "LISTEN . . . GOD IS TALKING"

a. Read Psalm 34:18–19.

b. Share what God taught you in chapter 6.

CHAPTER 7 "PRAYER'S NOURISHMENT"

a. Read Psalm 34:12–14.

b. Share from chapter 7.

D. In groups of three to four people:

Share any personal needs relating to chapters 4–7 and pray for each other.

E. As an entire group, review these chapters:

CHAPTER 8 "A LOVE GIFT"

a. Read Psalm 34:7.

b. Share what God showed you in chapter 8.

CHAPTER 9 "HONEST PRAISE"

a. Read Psalm 34:1–2.

b. Review the memory verse, Psalm 107:1 (TLB).

c. Share lessons gathered from chapter 9.

CHAPTER 10 "WHEN GOD DOESN'T ANSWER"

a. Read Psalm 34:4–7.

b. Share God's personal teaching to you from chapter 10.

CHAPTER 11 "WHAT DO YOU WANT WHEN YOU PRAY?"

a. Read Psalm 34:11.

b. Share personal lessons from chapter 11.

c. Sing together a praise song to God.

F. In groups of three to four people:

Share any needs you have in the areas dealt with in chapters 8–11 and pray for each other concerning these needs. Also share prayers of praise, thanking God for recent blessings.

G. As an entire group, review this chapter:

CHAPTER 12 "FOLLOWING THE PATTERN"

a. Share lessons God gave as you studied this chapter.

b. Pray the Lord's Prayer together as a closing prayer.

13

HELPS FOR LEADERS

PURPOSE OF THIS STUDY

Often the most difficult thing about prayer is establishing a consistent and meaningful prayer life. This study is directed to meet that need. This is not intended to be an all-inclusive study on prayer. Instead, the attention is on giving practical, honest aids in beginning or establishing a more effective prayer life.

Those in your group who have well-developed prayer lives will understand the need to begin with the basics. They, too, will be the first to admit that the basics are most easily neglected or forgotten. Enlist their help in praying for God's use of this study in your group. Their prayer support will make a difference.

The "Personal Prayer Discoveries" help—through prayer—to personalize the truths of each chapter. We spend more time reading or talking about prayer than we actually spend praying. As with walking or riding a bike, it's as you begin to participate in an activity that you become comfortable with the process.

The "Shared Discoveries in Prayer" further personalizes praying. These group meetings aren't intended as theological debates on the great questions concerning prayer. Rather, they are meant to help each person discover how prayer can become more personally meaningful.

GROUP LEADERS

Consider selecting women to lead the discussion when you divide into groups. (The small groups of two or three will not need leaders.) Group leaders' responsibilities would include: studying the discussion questions, leading a group discussion, and directing the small groups in prayer times. In preparation, leaders could pray for God's teaching power to be released in their groups.

GROUP DIVISION

Whenever suggested sizes of groups are noted, please feel free to adjust according to the particular needs, personalities, and overall size of your group.

LESSON PREPARATION

Perhaps the most important preparation is prayer. In addition to reading the chapter and the corresponding section in Helps for Leaders, allow God to guide you in considering the following:

1. Ask a few people to pray earnestly and specifically that God would use these weeks of study in the lives of those attending. If appropriate, you or someone from this prayer support group could pray by name for each

person attending that she would benefit from the experience.

2. Before each session:

   a. Pray in the room where you will meet for your group sessions.

   b. Ask God to fill your meeting room with His Presence.

   c. Ask God's Spirit to teach the women in your group.

3. Pray for each session:

   a. Ask God to speak His Words through you.

   b. Ask God to help everyone feel secure in His Presence so that each can be open to learning in the sessions.

   c. Pray about the specific topic you will discuss.

4. After each session:

   a. Thank God for His help.

   b. Thank God for specific things that happened.

   c. Ask God to personalize the truth of the session for each woman and to guide each one in her study of the next chapter.

5. If God so directs, you may want to do some kind of fasting in preparation for this study. This could be giving up a meal, or a series of meals or going without particular foods—whatever God directs. (Read Isaiah 58:6–9.)

TIME FOR YOUR SESSION

If the time allotted for your session doesn't allow you to do all of the Group Discoveries, please leave the prayer times intact. One of the main ways people learn to pray is by actually praying. Shorten the discussion time, if necessary.

CHAPTER 1

1. If your group is not well acquainted, have them introduce themselves and tell something personal, e.g., their favorite color. (Do this in pairs or small groups, if you have a large number attending.)

2. When the instructions are to pray silently, read the instructions to your group, and then take the lead in bowing your head to pray.

3. It's necessary to use a variety of Scriptures in this chapter. If locating these presents a problem to some of the members of your group, use whichever of the following would be appropriate:

   a. At the beginning of your discussion time, refer the entire group to the Bible's table of contents.

   b. Say something to make them comfortable, e.g., "The names of the Old Testament sound so foreign, it's easy to get lost—so let's help each other as we look up these Scripture references."

   c. Tell the group where the reference is located as you announce it: "near the front of the Bible," "this book is after Psalms," etc.

   d. You may have different people look up some of the Scriptures instead of everyone looking up each one; however, each looking up her own is helpful to the individual.

4. Make your notes on the discussion questions before the session.

5. Referring to **A #7:** Background material to aid your discussion leading is John 15 and 17.

6. Referring to **A #9:** Pray that God will bring meaningful instances to people's minds quickly. Have two of your own to *begin* with as your group thinks. If you feel it would be helpful, ask a couple of the women ahead of time to think of something they can share.

7. Referring to **B:** The small group of two or three is important to help everyone move slowly toward praying aloud together. For the same reason, each person will decide in this first session if she wishes to pray silently or aloud.

CHAPTER 2

1. Referring to **B:** The groups are large so those who are not Christians will feel comfortable.

2. Referring to the prayer time in **C #2:** Begin this the same way as the previous prayer time, with you praying first. Example: "Thank you for strength," etc. Since the women can pray more than once if they wish, be prepared to pray again if it takes your group a little time to pray freely.

3. Referring to the prayer time in **C #5:** Read the instructions aloud, then bow your head first. Your group will follow.

4. Referring to **C #9a:** If any of your group are adopted, or have adopted children or foster children, you might ask them ahead of time to share some of their feelings with the group.

5. Referring to **C #9b:** Include our need to be secure with God if we are to trust our needs, hurts, and loved ones to Him in prayer.

6. Be prepared to begin the sharing in **C #10,** or have one of your group prepared to begin.

7. Consider closing your meeting by singing together a song about God's love.

CHAPTER 3

1. Referring to **A #1:** Read aloud in unison the text of the verse listed to avoid the confusion of various translations.

2. Referring to **A #2a:** Examples: our problem, our schedule, a responsibility, the children, etc.

3. Referring to **A #2b:** Examples: focusing on a problem tends to make the problem bigger than God's power; focusing on our schedules tends to make us hurry, etc.

4. Referring to **C #2** and **#4:** Be prepared to begin the sharing yourself.

5. Referring to **C #5:** You could use a chalkboard or large tablet if you wish. Remember to discuss all three questions for each verse. Call on different ones to read each verse.

6. Referring to **C #7b:** It would be helpful if you had a song in mind.

7. Referring to **C #8c:** Either you can pray here, or call on someone who would be comfortable leading your group in prayer.

CHAPTER 4

1. You might begin by reviewing last week's memory verse.

2. Just before **A #2a,** read the meaning of "friend" from a dictionary or thesaurus.

3. Referring to **A #6d:** Include: Learn more about God, spend time with Him, ask God to help us believe He wants us to talk with Him, ask God to help us feel secure with Him.

4. Referring to **C #1b:** Include: It's necessary if we are to receive the kind of help we need, and if we are to become *intimate* with God.

5. Referring to **C #3:** Be prepared to share first.

6. Referring to **C #5:** Be prepared to begin.

CHAPTER 5

This chapter will help your group understand the importance of listening to God.

1. Referring to **A:** Read the Scripture provided (Luke 14:35b) to your group before you begin.

2. Referring to **A #2e:** Include: You feel you know the person better; are more comfortable with a person; more confident a person will care; will pay attention, will help.

3. Referring to **A #3:** Introduce the prayer, and bow your head to pray.

4. Referring to **A #5:** Call on someone to lead the group in prayer.

5. Referring to **A #7:** It would probably be helpful if you or someone else were ready to share first.

6. Referring to **B:** Allow the time left and the personalities of the women to determine the size of groups. The smaller the group the less time it will take. Also, if your group is not very comfortable sharing and praying, two to three would be a better size for this prayer time. (If

there is time and if your group is comfortable praying together, the larger group can be very meaningful.)

7. Consider closing with someone singing a song about God's voice or hearing God.

CHAPTER 6

1. Materials needed: For each person—pen/pencil, several sheets of paper, a Bible. For each group—a concordance, if available.

2. Referring to **A #4:** It might be most convenient to have your women sign up for a topic as they come into the session. To minimize confusion, work out ahead of time whatever method would be best for your group.

3. Referring to **A #5b:** Add any topics you know would be especially helpful for your group, preparing Scripture references to go with them before the session. (You will find a concordance helpful.)

4. Referring to **B:**

   a. Pass out to each group: Paper, pens, Bibles as needed and a concordance, if available.

   b. It would be helpful if you let them know how long they have to consider section B. Give a five- or ten-minute warning near the end. *Allow plenty of time.*

CHAPTER 7

1. Referring to **A #1:** Lead the group in this Scripture.

2. Referring to **A #2d:** Include: Believe God's will is best for us; start obeying; work on our attitudes; let God be in charge.

3. Referring to **C #1:** Read this Scripture aloud or call on someone else to. It's long, so the person will be more comfortable if she is a good reader.

4. Referring to **C #4:** Because we have so many excuses for the way we talk, it will be especially helpful to read these Scriptures from different versions of the Bible, giving new insights. The Living Bible's paraphrase of the proverbs listed will especially stimulate thinking.

5. Referring to **C #5:** Explain the prayer time, bow your head, and begin silently praying.

6. Referring to **C #6:** Be prepared to begin.

7. Referring to **C #7:** You might want to ask someone ahead to do this or call on someone comfortable both with praying and reading. Or you might do it yourself.

CHAPTER 8

1. Referring to **A #2:** Plan to spend considerable time here if people have much to share. It will help them believe in the importance of praying for others.

2. Referring to **C #1:** Read this yourself, or call on someone else to.

3. Referring to **C #2:** Direct this sharing and praying time. When people are finished praying aloud for a specific need, ask who else would like to share so the prayerful atmosphere is not disrupted.

4. Referring to **C #3:** Be prepared to close in prayer or call on someone else.

5. Referring to **C #4:** Remind your group members of this before they leave.

CHAPTER 9

1. Introduce the session by announcing that *no requests* will be presented to God. The session will center on praising Him.

2. Referring to **A #2:** You'll be referring to this list throughout. A chalkboard or large tablet may be helpful.

3. Referring to **A #4:** Be prepared to share first.

4. Referring to **C #2:** Include: God tells us to praise Him; God deserves praise; praising God reminds us of the kind of God we belong to; praising God reminds us of all God has done for us; praising God helps us dwell on the positive.

5. Referring to **C #4:** If there is time, encourage the women to share more than once but to share only one thing at a time. Keep all of this sharing in the context of *praise.*

CHAPTER 10

1. Referring to **A #2a:** Include: Doubting God's power; feeling God doesn't care; getting discouraged and giving up; doubting prayer in general.

2. Referring to **A #4a:** Include: Not disciplined in praying; get discouraged; forget to; impatient; have trouble believing that praying will accomplish anything.

3. Referring to **A #4c:** Include: When the prayer is answered or the situation resolved; when God directs us to; when we're just going through the motions and not really praying.

4. Referring to **A #6:** Introduce #6–8 as dealing with one example of disobedience—lack of forgiveness. That disobedience includes many things, but today you'll just be going over this one example.

5. Referring to **A #7a:** Include: They are not sorry; it really hurt us; we were right and they were wrong.

6. Referring to **C #1:** Be prepared to begin or ask someone else in advance.

7. Referring to **C #2:** Include: Give up on prayer or God; feel betrayed by God; get locked into our grief; act like it doesn't hurt us when it does so that the hurt festers.

CHAPTER 11

1. Referring to **A #8a:** Include: Our own way; our comfort; our happiness; the absence of all problems or difficulties.

2. Referring to **A #8b:** Include: Helps us to believe we should seek His purpose; helps us to want His will; helps us to learn how to fulfill His purpose for us.

3. Referring to **B:** Groups are larger here to make brainstorming easier. But if the women will brainstorm better in smaller groups, divide them that way.

4. Referring to **C #1:** Be prepared to share first.

5. Consider having a song about commitment at the end.

CHAPTER 12

We so often are touched by God and learn something special . . . then the learning and memory diminishes with the passage of time and the onslaught of activities. This chapter is for the women to remind, challenge, motivate, and further help each other. Have everyone look through the pages of the chapter being discussed to remind them of what was covered.